cracking
FRENCH
WINE

by Hugh Baker

For Rowan,
with thanks for all the
hard work this year, and
wishes for a Merry Christmas

Explore French wines
by grape variety

Hugh Baker

a **cracking.it** publication

Cracking French Wine
by Hugh Baker

© 2006 Hugh Thurlow Baker

a cracking.it publication
74 Wycliffe Road, London SW11 5QR, United Kingdom
Please visit us at http://www.cracking.it/

ISBN-10: 0-9544205-1-9
ISBN-13: 978-0-9544205-1-2

A Here+There production for cracking.it
Art Direction: Caz Hildebrand

Printed and bound in China

for Phoebe

ABOUT FRENCH WINE

Not only do the French make a lot of wine (one in four bottles worldwide), but they also make most of the world's greatest wines. France is lucky enough to have several near-perfect places to grow certain grapes. As a result, even non-drinkers have heard of Champagne, Bordeaux and Burgundy. These regions are famous because their best wines set the standard to which all other places aspire.

The French have also spent centuries matching grapes, soil types and techniques specifically for each part of the country. So it is hard for other places to make wines with the finesse that French wine can achieve.

Nearly all of the internationally recognisable grape varieties originally came from France, including Chardonnay, Cabernet Sauvignon, Pinot Noir, Merlot, Malbec and Sauvignon Blanc.

So if French wine is so great, why are people drinking less and less of it? Partly, this is because French wines are confusing. Variety may be the spice of life, but French wine takes this philosophy to a whole new level. French wines are usually labelled by where they come from, and not by the grapes they contain. Their wines are named after more than 300 places, most of which are so obscure and unpronounceable that they are only known by the local inhabitants and a few wine nerds.

Surely this is madness in today's competitive world? After all, isn't the taste of a wine primarily determined by the grape varieties from which it is made? Of course, other factors come into play such as the local weather conditions that year, soil type, altitude, hours of sunlight, how many bunches of grapes each vine is allowed to grow, or how the wine is made. But grape variety is still the single most recognisable factor in a wine, and people tend to remember the grape varieties they like. For example, you can instantly tell that a wine is made from Sauvignon Blanc grapes irrespective of where it comes from.

Wines from countries outside Europe capitalise on this and prominantly display grape varieties on their labels. This makes it much easier for the shopper. The French have made some moves to allow grape varieties on their labels, but where they do not do this the consumer has to recognise the place name on the bottle and then remember which grape varieties are grown there. Unless you are a wine geek (or you have this book!), it is unlikely you would buy a Limoux from France when looking for a full and fruity Chardonnay.

This problem is not only bad for the French wine trade: it is bad for consumers too, as we may all lose out on the sheer variety of experiences that only French wines can offer. In a world increasingly dominated by fast food chains, supermarkets, mass production and identikit high streets, French wines stand out. They should be enjoyed while there are French people dedicating their lives to creating the best wines that they can make.

This book is like a map. Use it to navigate your own journey through the world of French wines. Whether you are trawling the shelves for good value but lesser known wines, looking for something unusual, or just wanting to know what grape varieties are in what you are drinking, Cracking French Wine is there to help you make an informed choice.

The key to understanding French wine labels is the "appellation" system. An appellation is named after the place where the grapes are grown, and each one has regulations specifying grape varieties, grape-growing and wine-making techniques appropriate to the traditions, soil and climate of that place.

Each appellation is rated in a hierarchy, which is like a pyramid. There are four levels of appellation (this book covers the top two in detail).

1 At the top of the heap are the **Appellations d'Origine Contrôlées**, or AC wines. These include the most expensive wines in France. Wines at this level can easily be recognised because they all have the words "Appellation" and "Contrôlée" on their labels, usually with the appellation name squeezed between the two. Champagne is the only exception to this. At the AC level, almost every aspect of growing grapes and making wine is carefully regulated. Over half of French wine is rated AC.

2 The next level covers the **Vins Délimités de Qualité Supérieure**, or VDQS wines. This category is often seen as a holding status for wines awaiting promotion to AC status. Relatively little is produced – only 1% of all French wines are rated VDQS.

3 Next are the **Vins de Pays**, which are less tightly regulated. This relaxation of the rules allows many of the innovative New World wine-making techniques to be introduced to France, and so this category of wine is getting more interesting – and in some cases classic, like Mas de Daumas Gassac in the Languedoc. Often the grapes are displayed prominently on the labels.

4 At the bottom are the **Vins de Table**, which account for about 18% of France's wine production and are almost all consumed locally. These are not allowed to indicate grape variety or place of origin, so it is impossible to guess what grapes they contain.

Typically, a bottle of AC wine will display these elements:

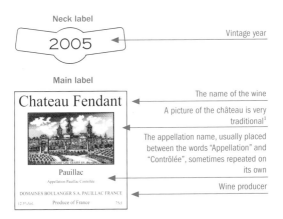

Neck label

2005 ← Vintage year

Main label

Chateau Fendant

The name of the wine

A picture of the château is very traditional[1]

The appellation name, usually placed between the words "Appellation" and "Contrôlée", sometimes repeated on its own

Pauillac
Appellation Pauillac Contrôlée

Wine producer

DOMAINES BOULANGER S.A. PAUILLAC FRANCE
12.5% Vol.   Produce of France   75cl

---

[1] A picture of the château should represent the actual wine estate – this picture is really of Cos d'Estournel, which is my favourite wine from Bordeaux

ABOUT THIS BOOK

The chapters in this book cover all of the wine-producing regions of France in turn.

Each chapter starts with a map of the region and a short introduction highlighting the key wine styles of the area and any idiosyncrasies you might encounter on a label.

The body of each chapter has a series of charts which group the appellations into columns by their principal grape varieties. Each column describes the primary taste characteristics and suggests successful food combinations. At the bottom of each column are other wines to try elsewhere in the book if you like the ones in this column.

At the end of each chapter is a section on recommended producers. Each of the producers listed have great reputations for making the best possible wines.

Finally, at the back of the book there is a combined index and glossary of terms, which lists all appellations and primary grape varieties.

What can you do with this pocket book?

1 **Find out which French wines are made from your favourite grape varieties.**
Look up the grape variety in the index, and follow suggested page links for the regions in which that grape is grown. For example, if you like Sauvignon Blancs, the index points you to Loire versions p57, Burgundy versions p34, or versions blended with Sémillon on p16.

2 **Discover those bargains that only the experts or locals know about.**
Look higher in the column chart containing the wine you are interested in finding cheaper alternatives for. For example, if you like white Sancerre, the column chart on p57 suggests Quincy and Reuilly are also Sauvignon Blancs from the Loire but are less expensive.

3 **Try new wines and grape varieties that are similar to those you already like.**
Follow the also try suggestions at the bottom of each column chart. For example, from Loire Sauvignon Blanc on p57, you might discover that Cour-Cheverny from the Romorantin grape is a great alternative with a grapefruit twist.

4 **Choose food to have with a particular bottle of French Wine.**
The description at the top of each column chart includes food matching suggestions.

KEY

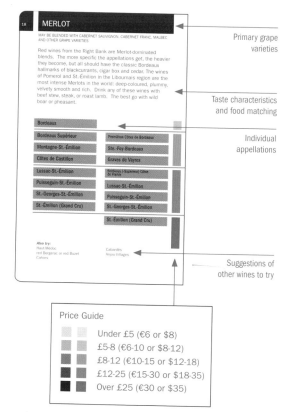

18

MERLOT

MAY BE BLENDED WITH CABERNET SAUVIGNON, CABERNET FRANC, MALBEC AND OTHER GRAPE VARIETIES

Red wines from the Right Bank are Merlot-dominated blends. The more specific the appellations get, the heavier they become, but all should have the classic Bordeaux hallmarks of blackcurrants, cigar box and cedar. The wines of Pomerol and St. Émilion in the Libournais region are the most intense Merlots in the world: deep-coloured, plummy, velvety smooth and rich. Drink any of these wines with beef stew, steak, or roast lamb. The best go with wild boar or pheasant.

Primary grape varieties

Taste characteristics and food matching

Bordeaux	
Bordeaux Supérieur	Premières Côtes de Bordeaux
Montagne-St.-Émilion	Ste.-Foy-Bordeaux
Côtes de Castillon	Graves de Vayres
Lussac-St.-Émilion	Bordeaux (-Supérieur) Côtes de France
Puisseguin-St.-Émilion	Lussac-St.-Émilion
St.-Georges-St.-Émilion	Puisseguin-St.-Émilion
St.-Émilion (Grand Cru)	St.-Georges-St.-Émilion
	St.-Émilion (Grand Cru)

Individual appellations

Also try:
Haut Medoc
red Bergerac or red Buzet
Cahors

Cabardés
Anjou Villages

Suggestions of other wines to try

Price Guide

	Under £5 (€6 or $8)
	£5-8 (€6-10 or $8-12)
	£8-12 (€10-15 or $12-18)
	£12-25 (€15-30 or $18-35)
	Over £25 (€30 or $35)

Please note:
Price ranges indicate expected retail price for a single 75cl bottle. Actual prices may be higher but price is not a reliable reflection of quality. Go for recommended producers before higher prices.

CONTENTS

Bordeaux (& satellites)   10

Burgundy (& Beaujolais)   26

Rhône   44

Loire   54

Alsace (& Lorraine)   68

Champagne   76

Jura & Savoie   80

South-West France   88

Languedoc-Roussillon   94

Provence   104

Corsica   108

Index   110

About us   124

Acknowledgements   126

BORDEAUX (& SATELLITE REGIONS)

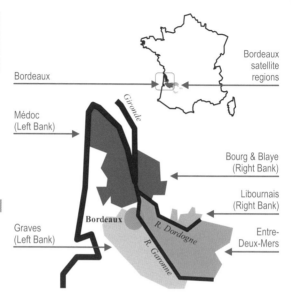

Bordeaux satellite regions

Bordeaux

Médoc (Left Bank)

Gironde

Bourg & Blaye (Right Bank)

Libournais (Right Bank)

Bordeaux

R. Dordogne

Entre-Deux-Mers

Graves (Left Bank)

R. Garonne

Bordeaux is to wine what Hollywood is to movies. Everyone there seems connected to the business; the product is global; there are the high-priced stars with egos to match, and many wannabes. Bordeaux produces more top quality and high-price wine than anywhere else in the world. Most other places simply cannot produce wines of similar complexity without severely restricting the number of grapes each vine is allowed to grow. In part, this is because Bordeaux is endowed with a near-perfect climate for growing wine grapes. The relatively cool climate, tempered by the Atlantic, and the poor gravelly soils force the vines to work hard to ripen their grapes, bringing out the best in the fruit. But that is not the whole story. Throughout Europe, making wine evolved as a hobby for monks, but in Bordeaux it has been a serious commercial enterprise for centuries. Even now when Bordeaux produces just over 10% of France's wine, it accounts for over 40% of French wine exports.

The most famous wines from châteaux like Lafite, Mouton-Rothschild and Pétrus may be household names, but most of us would need to win the lottery before being able to drink them. Why are some people willing to pay these prices? Partly it is due to very successful branding, and partly as a result of their longevity making them an attractive investment opportunity. But they would not be so highly prized if the taste of a mature wine from a good vintage was not so profound that you are still tasting it five minutes after the last sip, and so well balanced that you can recall the experience years later.

Six out of every seven bottles produced in Bordeaux are red. The reds are nearly all blends of several grapes, but primarily Cabernet Sauvignon and Merlot. Cabernet Sauvignon dominates the reds from Médoc and Graves (collectively known as the Left Bank) because it grows most successfully there, but most Bordeaux reds have more Merlot than any other grape. The proportions used vary from year to year depending on the weather and what each wine-maker is trying to achieve.

White wines are also blends, primarily of Sauvignon Blanc and Sémillon. Their styles may be anything from dry to intensely sweet. Often the labels do not indicate whether the wines are sweet or dry, but sweeter wines are often found in clear bottles, and dry wines in green bottles. Bordeaux is very famous for sweet white wines, especially those from Sauternes and Barsac in Graves. These are made from grapes affected by a naturally occurring form of mould known as "noble rot". In places with foggy mornings and sunny afternoons, this mould can make the grape skins porous and let the water evaporate from the juice, thus concentrating the sugars and flavours. The results can be nearly immortal – which is appropriate given the other-worldly taste of these wines: intense sweetness balanced by biting acidity, a long finish that alternates between honey, candied fruit and nuts.

There are many thousands of wine producers in Bordeaux – some say the only accurate list is the local telephone directory. To some degree, they all try to boost the price of their wines by hitching a ride on the reputations of the greatest châteaux, although often the association is tenuous. As a result, some labelling terms are helpful, others are just misleading:

1 **Grand Vin de Bordeaux** – often used, but does not mean that the wine is a great wine; it just means that the bottle is the right height!

2 **Supérieur** – does not necessarily mean that the wine is superior, only that the wine has a higher minimum alcohol content.

3 **Bordeaux** – at last, a word you can recognise! Sadly, any appellation with the word Bordeaux in it is the lowliest wine of the region – the most common is Bordeaux AC.

4 **Cru Classé** – this is the classification that includes all the famous names, like Latour and Lafite. Confusingly, Médoc, Graves and St.-Émilion all have different systems for classifying their châteaux (see box on page 22).

5 **Cru Bourgeois** – another classification system used in the Médoc. The original Cru Classé châteaux there were selected back in 1855, so the Cru Bourgeois classification was invented more recently to recognise other high performance châteaux. Top Cru Bourgeois can be easily as good or better than some Cru Classé châteaux.

BORDEAUX VINTAGES

Very good or great
Cabernet Sauvignon & Merlot reds: 1982, 1985, 1986, 1988, 1989, 1990, 1995, 1996, 2000, 2003, 2004.
Merlot reds: 1982, 1985, 1986, 1988, 1989, 1990, 1995, 1996, 1998, 1999, 2000.
Sweet whites: 1986, 1988, 1989, 1990, 1997, 2001, 2003.

Quite Good
Cabernet Sauvignon & Merlot reds: 1981, 1983, 1994, 1998, 1999, 2001, 2002.
Merlot blends: 1981, 1983, 1994, 2001, 2002, 2003, 2004.
Sweet whites: 1980, 1981, 1983, 1985, 1995, 1996, 1998, 1999, 2000, 2002.

Mixed or poor
Cabernet Sauvignon & Merlot reds: 1980, 1984, 1987, 1991, 1992, 1993, 1997.
Merlot blends: 1980, 1984, 1987, 1991, 1992, 1993, 1997
Sweet whites: 1982, 1984, 1987, 1991, 1992, 1993, 1994, 2004.

BORDEAUX APPELLATIONS

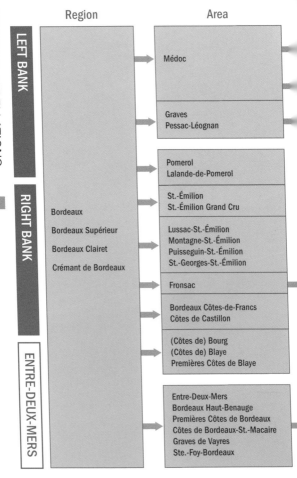

Region | **Area**

LEFT BANK

Médoc

Graves
Pessac-Léognan

RIGHT BANK

Bordeaux
Bordeaux Supérieur
Bordeaux Clairet
Crémant de Bordeaux

Pomerol
Lalande-de-Pomerol

St.-Émilion
St.-Émilion Grand Cru

Lussac-St.-Émilion
Montagne-St.-Émilion
Puisseguin-St.-Émilion
St.-Georges-St.-Émilion

Fronsac

Bordeaux Côtes-de-Francs
Côtes de Castillon

(Côtes de) Bourg
(Côtes de) Blaye
Premières Côtes de Blaye

ENTRE-DEUX-MERS

Entre-Deux-Mers
Bordeaux Haut-Benauge
Premières Côtes de Bordeaux
Côtes de Bordeaux-St.-Macaire
Graves de Vayres
Ste.-Foy-Bordeaux

District		Village

| **Haut Médoc** | → | Pauillac
Margaux
St.-Julien
St.-Éstephe |

| Listrac
Moulis |
| Cérons
Barsac
Sauternes |

Canon-Fronsac

Cadillac
Loupiac
Ste.-Croix-du-Mont

The first confusing thing about wines from Bordeaux is that they have appellations within appellations, several layers deep in places. Each layer represents a more specific description of where the grapes are grown than the level before. In general, the more specific the wines get, the higher the quality and price will be. Wines from a specific place that do not meet the higher quality standards may be sold as a less specific wine. Only the most basic wines are sold under the generic Bordeaux appellation, so if you are looking for a good bottle of Bordeaux, it probably won't say Bordeaux on the label!

SAUVIGNON BLANC & SÉMILLON

MAY BE BLENDED WITH MUSCADELLE

Dry whites from Bordeaux and its satellites are clean and crisp, and become more elegant and plump as they get more expensive. The crispness comes from Sauvignon Blanc, which Sémillon softens. Ideal with white fish, or semi-soft cheeses like Pont l'Evêque.

These white wines can all be made in both dry and sweeter styles. The convention is sweet wine in clear bottles, dry in green bottles. Drier wines are ideal with white fish dishes, the sweeter with fruit tart. The French drink the sweeter versions at weddings.

	Bordeaux (Sec)
	Bergerac (Sec/Moelleux)

Montravel	Bordeaux Supérieur
Côtes du Marmandais	Côtes de Duras (Sec/Moelleux)
Buzet	Bordeaux Haut-Benauge
(Côtes de) Blaye	Graves de Vayres
(Côtes de) Bourg	Ste.-Foy-Bordeaux
Entre-Deux-Mers	
Graves	

Premières Côtes de Blaye	Bordeaux (Supérieur) Côtes-de-Francs
Pessac-Léognan	

Also try:
white Sancerre
white Gaillac
white Châteauneuf-du-Pape

Also try:
Vouvray
Saumur
Alsace Riesling

BORDEAUX WHITE

USUALLY BLENDED WITH SAUVIGNON BLANC AND MUSCADELLE

Sweet white wines from Bordeaux are world renowned for their intensity, because the grapes are affected by the rare "noble rot" which concentrates the sugars and flavours. They can be overwhelmingly complex: honey, toast, hazelnuts, candied orange peel, peaches and lots more. They go beautifully with fruity desserts, but also foie gras or Roquefort cheese. The wines from Graves are the most intensely sweet, but those from other parts of Bordeaux and its satellites can also be wonderfully rich and full with soft honeyed noble rot character, and sometimes a little liquorice from sun-drying of the grapes on the vine. These go very well with fruit tarts or tarte tatin.

Côtes de Bordeaux-St.-Macaire	
Premières-Côtes-de-Bordeaux	

Cadillac	
Loupiac	
Ste.-Croix-du-Mont	
Graves Supérieur	Haut-Montravel/Côtes de Montravel
Cérons	Rosette

Bordeaux-Côtes-de-Francs Liquoreux	Saussignac
Barsac	Monbazillac
Sauternes	

Also try:

Bonnezeaux

Coteaux du Layon

Jurançon

sweet Alsace

Muscat de Beaumes-de-Venise

Gaillac Doux

BORDEAUX RED

MERLOT

MAY BE BLENDED WITH CABERNET SAUVIGNON, CABERNET FRANC, MALBEC AND OTHER GRAPE VARIETIES

Red wines from the Right Bank are Merlot-dominated blends. The more specific the appellations get, the heavier they become, but all should have the classic Bordeaux hallmarks of blackcurrants, cigar box and cedar. The wines of Pomerol and St.-Émilion in the Libournais region are the most intense Merlots in the world: deep-coloured, plummy, velvety smooth and rich. Drink any of these wines with beef stew, steak, or roast lamb. The best go with wild boar or pheasant.

Bordeaux

Bordeaux Supérieur	Premières Côtes de Bordeaux
Montagne-St.-Émilion	Ste.-Foy-Bordeaux
Côtes de Castillon	Graves de Vayres

Lussac-St.-Émilion	Bordeaux (-Supérieur) Côtes de Francs
Puisseguin-St.-Émilion	Fronsac
St.-Georges-St.-Émilion	(Côtes-) Canon-Fronsac
St.-Émilion (Grand Cru)	Lalande-de-Pomerol

Pomerol

Also try:
Haut-Médoc
red Bergerac or red Buzet
Cahors

Cabardès
Anjou-Villages

BORDEAUX RED

MAY BE BLENDED WITH CABERNET FRANC, MALBEC, PETIT VERDOT AND OTHER GRAPE VARIETIES

The wines of the Left Bank cemented the reputation of Bordeaux as the premier wine region of the world. The Cabernet Sauvignon provides blackcurrants and cigar boxes, and a strong tannic backbone that takes time to soften, while Merlot is plummy and makes the wines softer and rounder. The red wines of Graves are more "earthy" then those of Médoc, and can have a touch of tobacco or violets on the nose. All of these wines go very well with red meat dishes such as roast lamb, or rabbit casserole. Or you can skewer a strawberry on a fork and dunk it into a glass.

	Blaye/Blayais
	Premières Côtes de Blaye
Médoc	(Côtes de) Bourg/Bourgeais

Haut-Médoc	Graves
Listrac (-Médoc)	
Moulis (-en-Médoc)	

St.-Julien	Pessac-Léognan
St.-Estèphe	Margaux
	Pauillac

Also try:

red Bergerac or red Buzet	red Bourgueil
Cahors	red Côte de Nuits
Cabardès	red Hermitage
St.-Émilion	Moulin-à-Vent

BORDEAUX RED

MERLOT, CABERNETS SAUVIGNON & FRANC

MAY BE BLENDED WITH TANNAT AND FER

These wines from the Bordeaux satellite regions are very much like other Bordeaux reds. They might not reach the same heights, but they have rich, full fruit, and are definitely much better value at each price level. The addition of local grapes gives them a slightly rustic flavour, but they are still capable of great finesse and charm. Drink them with dark red meat dishes like beef stroganoff or lamb casserole.

MALBEC

MAY BE BLENDED WITH MERLOT, TANNAT AND JURANÇON NOIR

The most famous wine from the Bordeaux satellite regions is the "black wine" of Cahors, which gets its nickname from the inky qualities of the Mablec grape. These wines are silky, with full plummy blackcurrant fruit, and can have an aroma of violets. These wines are excellent with beef stroganoff, or hot cooked ham.

PRICE

Côtes du Brulhois	
Coteaux de Quercy	
Bergerac	Cahors
Côtes de Duras	
Côtes du Marmandais	
Côtes de Bergerac	
Buzet	
Pécharmant	

Also try:
red Pessac-Léognan
Haut-Médoc
red Gaillac
Cahors

Also try:
Touraine Cot
Haut-Médoc

CABERNET SAUVIGNON & MERLOT

MAY BE BLENDED WITH CABERNET FRANC AND OTHER GRAPES

These pink wines from Bordeaux are fruitier and less tannic than the reds, although they use the same grape varieties. They go very well with cold meats for lunch. Some wines are labelled as "clairet", which is somewhere between a dark rosé and a light red. The French word clairet is the origin of the British use of the word "claret" to describe red wines of Bordeaux.

CABERNET FRANC & MERLOT

MAY BE BLENDED WITH MALBEC

These pink wines from the Bordeaux satellite regions are easy drinking, fresh and light, firmly crisp, and full of ripe fruit. Lovely on their own as an aperitif.

BORDEAUX PINK

Bordeaux (Rosé)

Côtes du Brulhois

Coteaux de Quercy

Bordeaux Supérieur Rosé

Bordeaux (Supérieur) Clairet

Bergerac

Côtes de Duras

Côtes du Marmandais

Buzet

Also try:
pink Buzet
pink St.-Nicolas-de-Bourgueil
Rosé de Loire
red Bordeaux

Also try:
Bordeaux Rosé
pink St.-Nicolas-de-Bourgueil
pink Côtes du Frontonnais
red Bergerac

BORDEAUX SPARKLING

SÉMILLON, SAUVIGNON BLANC & MUSCADELLE	CABERNET SAUVIGNON & MERLOT
These white sparkling wines are modest, light-bodied sparklers. Mix with cassis or orange juice for a cheap Kir Royale or Bucks Fizz.	These pink sparklers have not much more body than sparkling white Bordeaux. These wines could be much better if the Bordeaux appellation regulations allowed white grapes into the blend.
Crémant de Bordeaux	Crémant de Bordeaux
Also try: white Crémant de Bourgogne white Crémant de Loire white Touraine Mousseux	**Also try:** pink Crémant de Bourgogne pink Crémant d'Alsace

BORDEAUX CLASSIFICATIONS

Bordeaux has several systems for ranking their châteaux (words found on bottles are highlighted):

- 1855 Classification of Médoc "Cru Classé" (classed growth) red wines: top is Premier Cru Classé, then four other Cru Classé levels
- The Médoc has a second classification system, called Cru Bourgeois: best wines are marked Exceptionnel, very good are marked Supérieur, and the others are just plain Cru Bourgeois
- 1855 Classification of sweet white wines from Sauternes and Barsac in Graves, from the top: Premier Cru Supérieur (just Château d'Yquem), Premier Cru, and Deuxième Cru
- Red and white wines of Graves can be Cru Classé too under their own system, although Haut-Brion was actually included on the 1855 Médoc list
- St.-Émilion has a Grand Cru Classé system, whose top wines are Premier Grand Cru Classé

Dry Sémillon & Sauvignon Blanc whites (page 16):
EDM *Entre-Deux-Mers;* G *Graves;* P-L *Pessac-Léognan.*
Ch d'**Archambeau** (G), Ch la **Blancherie** (G), Ch **Bonnet**
(EDM), Ch **Carbonnieux** (P-L[a]), Ch de **Chantegrive** (G),
Dom de **Chevalier** (P-L[a]), Clos **Floridène** (G), Ch **Couhins-
Lurton** (P-L[a]), Ch de **Fieuzal** (P-L[a]), Ch **Grossombre** (EDM),
Ch **Haut-Brion** (P-L[a]), Ch **Laville Haut-Brion** (P-L[a]), Ch la
Louvière (P-L) and Ch **Olivier** (P-L).
Notes: [a] *Cru Classé*

Sweet Sémillon-based whites (page 17):
BC *Barsac;* C *Cérons;* H-M *Haut-Montravel;* LC *Loupiac;*
MC *Monbazillac;* R *Rosette;* CDM *Ste.-Croix-du-Mont;* S
Sauternes; SC *Saussignac*
l'**Ancienne Cure** (MC), Ch de **Cérons** (C), Ch le **Chabrier**
(SC), Ch **Climens** (BC[b]), **Clos Jean** (LC), Ch de **Contancie**
(R), Ch **Coutet** (BC[b]), Ch du **Cros** (LC), Ch **Doisy-Daëne**
(BC[c]), Ch **Doisy-Védrines** (BC[c]), Ch de **Fargues** (S), Ch
Gilette (S), **Grand Enclos du Château de Cérons** (C),
La **Grande Maison** (MC), Ch **Guiraud** (S[b]), Ch **Lafaurie-
Payraguey** (S[b]), Ch **Loubens** (CDM), Ch de **Malle** (S[c]),
Ch **Lousteau-Vieil** (CDM), Ch la **Maurigne** (SC), Ch
Miaudoux (SC), Ch **Puy Servain** (H-M), Ch **Raymond-
Lafon** (S), Ch **Rayne-Vigneau** (S[b]), Ch de **Ricaud** (LC), Ch
Rieussec (S[b]), Ch **Sigelas-Rabaud** (S[b]), Ch **Suduiraut** (S[b]),
Ch des **Tastes** (CDM), Ch **Tirecul-la-Gravière** (MC), Ch la
Tour Blanche (S[b]) and Ch d'**Yquem** (S[a]).
Notes: [a] *Premier Cru Supérieur,* [b] *Premier Cru,* [c] *Deuxième
Cru*

Merlot-based reds (page 18):
CdeB *Premières Côtes de Bordeaux;* CdeC *Côtes de Castil-
lon;* CdeF *Bordeaux Côtes de Francs;* C-F *Canon-Fronsac;*
F *Fronsac;* LdeP *Lalande-de-Pomerol;* MStE *Montagne-St.-
Émilion;* POM *Pomerol;* StE *St.-Émilion.*
Ch d'**Aiguilhe** (Cde[c]), Ch l'**Angelus** (StE[b]), Ch l'**Arrosée**

(StE[c]), Ch **Ausone** (StE[a]), Ch **Beau-Séjour Bécot** (StE[b]), Ch **Beauregard** (POM), Ch **Belair** (StE[b]), Ch de **Belcier** (CdeC), Ch le **Bon Pasteur** (POM), Ch **Canon la Gaffe-lière** (StE[c]), Ch **Cap de Faugères** (CdeC), Ch **Certan-de-May** (POM), Ch **Cheval Blanc** (StE[a]), Ch **Clinet** (POM), **Clos Fourtet** (StE[b]), Ch la **Conseillante** (POM), Ch **Croix-Beauséjour** (MStE), Ch la **Dominique** (StE[c]), Ch l'**Eglise-Clinet** (POM), Ch l'**Enclos** (POM), Ch l'**Evangile** (POM), Ch **Figeac** (StE[b]), Ch la **Fleur de Boüard** (LdeP), Ch la **Fleur de Gay** (POM), Ch la **Fleur Pétrus** (POM), Ch **Fontenil** (F), Ch de **Francs** (CdeF), Ch du **Gaby** (C-F), Ch la **Gaffelière** (StE[b]), Ch le **Gay** (POM), Ch **Gazin** (POM), Ch **Grand-Mouëys** (CdeB), Ch **Hosanna** (POM), Ch **Laclaverie** (CdeF), Ch **Lafleur** (POM), Ch **Larmande** (StE[c]), Ch **Latour à Pomerol** (POM), Ch **Lezongars** (CdeB), Ch **Magdelaine** (StE[b]), Ch **Monbousquet** (StE), Ch la **Mondotte** (StE), Ch **Moulin-Haut-Laroque** (F), Ch **Pavie** (StE[b]), Ch **Pavie Macquin** (StE[c]), Ch **Petit Village** (POM), Ch **Pétrus** (POM), le **Pin** (POM), Ch la **Prade** (CdeF), Ch **Puygueraud** (CdeF), Ch Reynon (CdeB), Ch **Robin** (CdeC), Ch **Roudier** (MStE), Ch **Tertre-Rôteboeuf** (StE), Ch **Trotanoy** (POM), Ch **Valandraud** (StE), Ch la **Vieille-Cure** (F) and Vieux-Château-Certan (POM).
Notes: [a] St.-Émilion Premier Grand Cru Classé A,
[b] St.-Émilion Premier Grand Cru Classé B,
[c] St.-Émilion Grand Cru Classé

Cabernet Sauvignon & Merlot blends (page 19):
BG Côtes de Bourg; BY Blaye or Premières Côtes de Blaye; HM Haut-Médoc; LC Listrac; M Margaux; MC Médoc; ML Moulis; P Pauillac; P-L Pessac-Léognan; StES St.-Estèphe; StJ St.Julien

Ch d'**Angludet** (M[d]), Ch **Bahans Haut-Brion** (P-L, second wine of Haut-Brion), Ch **Batailley** (P[b]), Ch **Branaire-Ducru** (StJ[b]), Ch **Brane-Cantenac** (M[b]), Ch **Calon-Ségur** (StES[b]), Ch **Cantemerle** (HM[b]), Ch **Carmes-Haut-Brion**

(P-L), Ch **Chasse-Spleen** (ML[c]), Dom de **Chevalier** (P-L[b]), **Clos du Marquis** (StJ, second wine of Léoville-Las-Cases), Ch **Cos d'Estournel** (StES[b]), Ch **Ducru-Beaucaillou** (StJ[b]), Ch **Durfort-Vivens** (M[b]), Ch de **Fieuzal** (P-L[b]), Les **Forts de Latour** (P, second wine of Latour), Ch **Fougas** (BG), Ch **Grand-Puy-Lacoste** (P[b]), Ch **Gruaud-Larose** (StJ[b]), Ch **Haut-Bages-Libéral** (P[b]), Ch **Haut-Bailly** (P-L[b]), Ch **Haut-Batailley** (P[b]), Ch **Haut-Bertinerie** (BY), Ch **Haut-Brion** (P-L[a]), Ch d'**Issan** (M[b]), Ch **Kirwan** (M[b]), Ch **Labégorce-Zédé** (M[c]), Ch **Lafite-Rothschild** (P[a]), Ch **Lafon-Rochet** (StES[b]), Ch **Lagrange** (StJ[b]), Ch la **Lagune** (HM[b]), Ch **Langoa-Barton** (StJ[b]), Ch **Latour** (P[a]), Ch **Léoville-Barton** (StJ[b]), Ch **Léoville-Las-Cases** (StJ[b]), Ch **Léoville-Poyferré** (StJ[b]), Ch la **Louvière** (P-L), Ch **Lynch-Bages** (P[b]), Ch **Margaux** (M[a]), Ch la **Mission-Haut-Brion** (P-L[b]), Ch **Montrose** (StES[b]), Ch **Mouton-Rothschild** (P[a]), Ch les **Ormes de Pez** (StES[c]), Ch **Palmer** (M[b]), Ch **Pape-Clément** (P-L[b]), Ch de **Pez** (StES[c]), Ch **Phélan-Ségur** (StES[c]), Ch **Pichon-Longueville** (P[b]), Ch **Pichon-Longueville-Comtesse-de-Lalande** (P[b]), Ch **Potensac** (HM[c]), Ch **Pontet-Canet** (P[b]), Ch **Poujeaux** (ML[c]), Ch **Rauzan-Ségla** (M[b]), **Roc des Cambes** (BG), Ch **St.-Pierre** (StJ[b]), Ch **Sociando-Mallet** (HM), Ch **Talbot** (StJ[b]), Ch **Tayac** (BG), Ch du **Tertre** (M[b]), Ch des **Tourtes** (BY) and Ch de **Villegorge** (HM[d]).

Notes: [a] *Premier Cru Classé*, [b] *Cru Classé*, [c] *Cru Bourgeois Exceptionnel*, [d] *Cru Bourgeois Supérieur*

Malbec reds (page 20):
All *Cahors*
Ch la **Caminade**, Ch du **Cayrou**, Ch du **Cèdre**, Clos **Triguedina**, Ch la **Coustarelle**, Ch **Haut-Monplaisir**, Ch **Lagrézette**, Ch **Lamartine**, Les **Laquets**, **Primo Palatum** and Ch la **Reyne**.

(Abbreviations: Ch for Château, Dom for Domaine)

BURGUNDY (& BEAUJOLAIS)

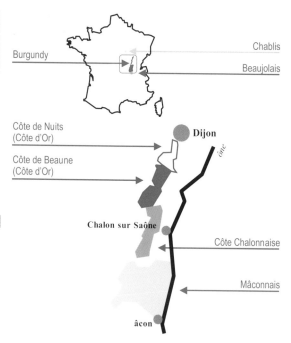

Chablis

Burgundy

Beaujolais

Côte de Nuits
(Côte d'Or)

Côte de Beaune
(Côte d'Or)

Dijon

ône

Chalon sur Saône

Côte Chalonnaise

Mâconnais

âcon

If "keep it simple, stupid" is a plea for modern life,
Burgundian wine is the antithesis. No other consumer
product in the world intentionally makes itself so
mystifying.

Burgundy's two most famous grapes, Chardonnay and
Pinot Noir, have spread around the world to become truly
international, and yet Burgundy still sets the standard

for everyone else to beat. A mature Pinot Noir from the Côte de Nuits can deliver an orgasmic hit that leaves you speechless with appreciation. Equally, Chardonnays from the Côte de Beaune can be so mind-bendingly complex that you quickly run out of words to describe them. Unfortunately such experiences come at a high price, but high prices are no guarantee of such experiences.

How can Burgundy reach such heights? Firstly, generations of wine-makers have spent centuries obsessively matching grape varieties to soil types. Where limestone predominates, Chardonnay is planted; Pinot Noir where the soil is marl and clay. Secondly, they have divided the Côte d'Or, Chablis and Côte Chalonnaise districts into a patchwork quilt of named vineyards, which they have graded by their potential for greatness based on micro-climate and soil (the best vineyards are called "Grand Cru" or great growth, and the very good are called "Premier Cru" or first growth).

So far, so good. But Burgundy can also be hugely frustrating. To start with, there are more appellations here than any other region in France. As in Bordeaux, there is a hierarchy of increasingly specific appellations: the regional wines (all of which have "Bourgogne" in their name), some district appellations, and many village appellations. However, Burgundian appellations do not stop there: in the Côte d'Or, Grand Cru vineyards are appellations in their own right. Identifying a Premier Cru wine is harder: they may say "Premier Cru" or "1er Cru" on the label next to the village name, but not necessarily. They may also be sold under the village appellation with the name of the vineyard in the same size letters as the village name.

So, if you see a bottle where the vineyard name is half the size of the village name, this is not a Premier Cru!

To make matters worse, Napoleonic inheritance law has led to extreme fragmentation of ownership of the vineyards. Some people own only a single row of vines. So, there are thousands growers and wine-makers to choose from, and correspondingly the quantities of each wine made is generally small. This means that if you find a wine you really like you may never be able to find it again.

The final kicker is that Burgundy produces only half what Bordeaux produces and the demand exceeds supply. This means that wines from Burgundy are relatively expensive. It also means that growers are guaranteed to sell their grapes, irrespective of their quality. For these reasons, the Grand Cru vineyards of the Côte d'Or are the most expensive agricultural land on the planet.

All in all, blindly experimenting with Burgundy can be an expensive and frustrating business. So how do you maximise your chances of getting a good wine? One approach is to go to Burgundy, do a tour of local wine cellars, see what you like and buy it. Another is to always choose a reputable producer, and buy any of the wines they make. You are better off buying a village wine from a decent producer than a Grand Cru from a bad one. However, there is no official classification of good producers, so without prior experience or a guide buying Burgundy can be a random walk. See pages 42 and 43 for a list of reputable producers. Alternatively, wines from the Côte Chalonnaise or Mâconnais regions tend to be more modestly priced than those from the Côte d'Or.

Chablis offers famously steely and mineral Chardonnays to contrast with the fuller wines from the Côte d'Or.

Finally, Beaujolais is different from the rest of Burgundy. The granite-based soils there get the best out of the Gamay grape. Beaujolais Nouveau is probably the most famous example of wine made there, but certainly not the best. The best ten vineyard sites are called the "Cru Beaujolais", which coax more intensity from the Gamay grape than anywhere else in the world.

BURGUNDY VINTAGES

Very good or great
Côte d'Or red: 1989, 1990, 1995, 1996, 1997, 1999, 2002, 2003.
Côte d'Or white: 1982, 1983, 1985, 1986, 1988, 1989, 1990, 1992, 1995, 1996, 1997, 1998, 1999, 2000, 2002.
Beaujolais: 1999, 2000, 2003.

Quite Good
Côte d'Or red: 1985, 1988, 1991, 1993, 1998, 2000.
Côte d'Or white: 1981, 1984, 1987, 1993, 1994, 2001, 2004.
Beaujolais: 1990, 1991, 1993, 1994, 1995, 1996, 1997, 1998, 2002, 2004.

Mixed or poor
Côte d'Or red: 1980, 1981, 1982, 1983, 1984, 1986, 1987 1992,, 1994, 2001, 2004.
Côte d'Or white: 1980, 1991, 2003.
Beaujolais: 1992, 2001.

CÔTE D'OR APPELLATIONS

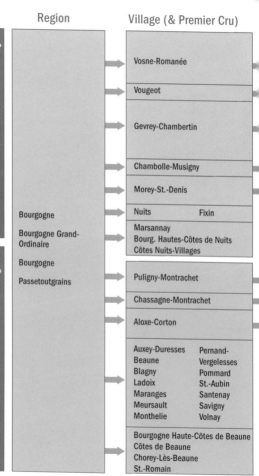

Region   **Village (& Premier Cru)**

CÔTE DE NUITS

CÔTE DE BEAUNE

Vosne-Romanée

Vougeot

Gevrey-Chambertin

Chambolle-Musigny

Morey-St.-Denis

Nuits   Fixin

Marsannay
Bourg. Hautes-Côtes de Nuits
Côtes Nuits-Villages

Bourgogne

Bourgogne Grand-
Ordinaire

Bourgogne

Passetoutgrains

Puligny-Montrachet

Chassagne-Montrachet

Aloxe-Corton

Auxey-Duresses   Pernand-
Beaune   Vergelesses
Blagny   Pommard
Ladoix   St.-Aubin
Maranges   Santenay
Meursault   Savigny
Monthelie   Volnay

Bourgogne Haute-Côtes de Beaune
Côtes de Beaune
Chorey-Lès-Beaune
St.-Romain

Grand Cru Vineyard

Echézeaux	Richebourg
Grand Echézeaux	La Romanée
Romanée-St.-Vivant	Romanée-Conti
La Grand Rue	La Tâche

Clos de Vougeot	

Chapelle-Chambertin	
Chambertin-Clos de Bèze	Ruchottes-Chambertin
Charmes-Chambertin	Chambertin
Mazoyères-Chambertin	Griottes-Chambertin
Mazy-/Mazis-Chambertin	Latricères-Chambertin

Bonnes Mares	Musigny

Clos du Lambrays	Clos St.-Denis
Clos de la Roche	Clos de Tart

Bâtard-Montrachet	Bienvenues-Bâtard-Montrachet
Chevalier-Montrachet	(Le) Montrachet

Criots-Bâtard-Montrachet	

Charlemagne	Corton-Charlemagne
Corton	

The wines of Côte d'Or in Burgundy have the most complicated appellation system in the world. The key to understanding the appellations is recognising whether the wine is a village wine, a Premier Cru or a Grand Cru. Premiers Crus are better sites than villages, and Grands Crus are better than Premiers Crus. But this is only the potential of the wine. Sadly, bad growers and wine-makers exist, so the recommended producers are a more reliable indicator of quality than appellation (see pages 42 and 43 for a list).

BURGUNDY WHITE

The white wines of Burgundy are famous because the Côte de Beaune produces the most wonderful and powerful Chardonnays in the world. They are all pale and dry, and capable of extraordinary intensity and complexity: hints of apple, melon, fig, nuts, butter, toastiness, creaminess, and some vanilla-spice. With age, they become honeyed and mellow. They also come in a dizzying range of tastes. Meursault, Aloxe-Corton, Auxey-Duresses and Savigny-Lès-Beaune are buttery, fat and rich. Puligny-Montrachet, St.-Aubin, Beaune and Chassagne-Montrachet are almost steely, and smoky with great finesse.

Petit Chablis	Mâcon (Supérieur)
Chablis	Givry
Bourgogne Hautes-Côtes de Nuits	Bourgogne Hautes-Côtes de Beaune
Côte de Nuits Villages	Côte de Beaune
Chablis Premier Cru	Beaune (Premier Cru)
Marsannay (La Côte)	Auxey-Duresses (Premier Cru)
Fixin (Premier Cru)	Chorey-Lès-Beaune
Morey-St.-Denis (Premier Cru)	Ladoix (Premier Cru)
Nuits-St.-Georges (Premier Cru)	Maranges (Premier Cru)
Vougeot (Premier Cru)	Meursault(-Blagny) (Premier Cru)
Chablis Grand Cru	Puligny-Montrachet (Premier Cru)
(Le) Musigny Grand Cru	Chassagne-Montrachet (Premier Cru)
	Chevalier-Montrachet Grand Cru

Also try:

Côtes du Jura Chardonnay   white Châteauneuf-du-Pape

Corton-Charlemagne is the most decadent Chardonnay anywhere, and all Grand Crus with Montrachet in their names are all deeply elegant and complex, with masses of toasty, floral, creamy, nutty, spicy and honey to test your taste-buds. Only a tiny amount of wine from the Côte de Nuits is white. Chablis wines are classically lean, mineral and austere. Village and Premier Cru wines are fabulous with white fish, or snails. Grand Cru wines deserve to be served with the most sumptuous meals of fish or white meat, like wild salmon, scallops, lobster or roast veal.

Mâcon Villages	Viré-Clessé
Mercurey	St.-Véran
Montagny	Pouilly-Loché
Rully	Pouilly-Vinzelles
Monthelie (Premier Cru)	Pouilly-Fuissé
Pernand-Vergelesses (Premier Cru)	Givry (Premier Cru)
St.-Aubin (Premier Cru)	Mercurey (Premier Cru)
St.-Romain	Montagny (Premier Cru)
Santenay (Premier Cru)	Rully (Premier Cru)
Savigny-Lès-Beaune (Premier Cru)	Aloxe-Corton (Premier Cru)
Bienvenues-Bâtard-Montrachet Grand Cru	(Le) Corton Grand Cru
Criots-Bâtard-Montrachet Grand Cru	Corton-Charlemagne Grand Cru
Bâtard-Montrachet Grand Cru	(Le) Montrachet Grand Cru

Limoux   white Hermitage

CHARDONNAY & ALIGOTÉ

Despite the addition of Aligoté, which is lighter-bodied than Chardonnay, Beaujolais whites have a little more body than Mâconnais whites. They are still crisp and light, though, and are great for relaxing in front of the TV or with chicken dishes.

Beaujolais (Blanc)

Beaujolais Supérieur

Coteaux du Lyonnais

Beaujolais-Villages

Also try:
Bourgogne Aligoté-Bouzeron
white Cheverny
Muscadet de Sèvre-et-Maine

SAUVIGNON BLANC

This is the only Sauvignon Blanc grown in Burgundy, and is really a refugee from the Loire. These wines are light and crisp, with classic Sauvignon Blanc notes of cut grass and gooseberry. They are wonderful with rich chicken dishes, or river fish such as trout.

St.-Bris

Also try:
white Sancerre
white Cheverny
Cour-Cheverny

ALIGOTÉ

Aligoté wines are light and refreshing. The best are from Bouzeron, where the wines have a rich and spicy character and are great with shellfish, otherwise just mix with cassis to make kir.

Bourgogne Aligoté (Bouzeron)

Bourgogne Grand-Ordinaire

Also try:
Beaujolais Blanc
Alsace Tokay Pinot Gris

CHARDONNAY & PINOT BLANC

Basic, dry and crisp. They are usually quite expensive for what they are, although the best examples are mainly Chardonnay and say so on the label. Drink on their own or with chicken dishes.

Bourgogne (Blanc)(village name)

PRICE

Also try:
Bourgogne Aligoté
Mâcon-Villages

Gamay is grown in the southern part of Burgundy. Basic Beaujolais reds are light-bodied with almost no tannin, having been fermented in their skins under a blanket of carbon dioxide. They have vibrant fruit flavours, and notes of pear, banana and nail polish, and are light lunchtime quaffers, maybe with a cold buffet or sandwich. Beaujolais Nouveau is sold from the third Thursday in November. However, not all Gamays are like Nouveau! The best come from Cru Beaujolais sites, which have the granite soil needed to grow great Gamay grapes. These wines have intense fruit flavours of strawberries and raspberries, with spicy-rich oak, floral aromas, and sometimes a meatiness, and will improve with age. They are fantastic partners for terrine or cold meats: cold duck, ham or cold roast pork. Their relatively low tannin also means they go very well with soft cheeses such as Brie and Camembert. The Mâcon reds have a harder edge as they are grown on limestone not granite.

PRICE

Beaujolais Nouveau/Primeur	Mâcon (village name)
Beaujolais (village name)	Mâcon Supérieur
Beaujolais Supérieur	Chiroubles (Cru Beaujolais)
Beaujolais-Villages	Côtes de Brouilly (Cru Beaujolais)
Régnié (Cru Beaujolais)	Juliénas (Cru Beaujolais)
Coteaux du Lyonnais	Chénas (Cru Beaujolais)
Brouilly (Cru Beaujolais)	St.-Amour (Cru Beaujolais)
Fleurie (Cru Beaujolais)	Morgon (Cru Beaujolais)
	Moulin-à-Vent (Cru Beaujolais)

Also try:
red Cheverny
Anjou Gamay
red Côte du Forez

Vin de Savoie Gamay
red Côtes de Millau
Côtes du Jura Poulsard

Côte de Nuits

The red wines of the Côte de Nuits in the north of Burgundy are the world's firmest, weightiest Pinot Noirs. They can be rich, elegant and fragrant, full of soft red fruit flavours like red cherries and raspberries, with hints of chocolate, spice and strawberries in good vintages. Although they have much softer tannins than Bordeaux reds, there is enough structure and fruit for them to age well. Premiers Crus from Côte de Nuits can age for up to 20 years, and some Grands Crus such as La Tâche and Romanée-Conti can go 30 years or more. As they age, these wines can develop hints of vegetables and farmyards.

Bourgogne Hautes-Côtes de Nuits	Côte de Nuits Villages
Fixin (Premier Cru)	Chambolle-Musigny (Premier Cru)
	Morey-St.-Denis (Premier Cru)
Clos (de) Vougeot Grand Cru	Chapelle-Chambertin Grand Cru
Clos du Lambrays Grand Cru	Ruchottes-Chambertin Grand Cru
Clos de la Roche Grand Cru	Griottes-Chambertin Grand Cru
Clos St.-Denis Grand Cru	Latricères-Chambertin Grand Cru
Clos de Tart Grand Cru	Chambertin Grand Cru
	Chambertin-Clos de Bèze Grand Cru

Also try:
red Côte de Beaune   red Sancerre
red Mercurey or red Rully   red Alsace

The wines from Vosne-Romanée and its Grand Crus are renowned for being the greatest expression of Pinot Noir. In particular, Domaine de la Romanée-Conti makes wines of unparalleled power and opulence – the memory of the taste experience (and the sincere thanks of your companions) will live longer that it takes to pay off the credit card bill. To get the most out of drinking these wines, have them with dark meat casseroles, classic roast meat like beef, duck or lamb.

Marsannay (La Côte)

Vougeot (Premier Cru)	Gevrey-Chambertin (Premier Cru)
Nuits (-St.-Georges) (Premier Cru)	Vosne-Romanée (Premier Cru)

Mazoyères-/Charmes-Chambertin Grand Cru	La Grand Rue Grand Cru
Mazy-/Mazis-Chambertin Grand Cru	Romanée-St.-Vivant Grand Cru
Bonnes Mares Grand Cru	Richebourg Grand Cru
(Le) Musigny Grand Cru	La Romanée Grand Cru
Échezeaux Grand Cru	La Tâche Grand Cru
Grand Échezeaux Grand Cru	Romanée-Conti Grand Cru

Cru Beaujolais
red Cheverny

Haut-Médoc
red Bourgueil

BURGUNDY RED

Côte de Beaune

Although endowed with more appellations for red wine than the Côte de Nuits, the Côte de Beaune is not famed for its reds. They are still great wines, with masses of raspberry and red cherry fruit and hints of spice, but they are generally less concentrated, lighter and less elegant than Côte de Nuits reds. Le Corton is the only Grand Cru for red wines here, and is the only wine capable of achieving the greatness of Côte de Nuits – weighty and sublime. Pommard and Beaune are the deepest and fullest flavoured, and Santenay and Volnay are the lightest. These wines go well with roast beef, duck or lamb.

Côte de Beaune Villages	
Bourgogne Hautes-Côtes de Beaune	**Côte de Beaune**
Chorey-Lès-Beaune (Côtes de Beaune)	Meursault (Côtes de Beaune) (Premier Cru)
St.-Romain (Côtes de Beaune)	Monthélie (Côtes de Beaune) (Premier Cru)
Maranges (Côtes de Beaune) (Premier Cru)	Pernand-Vergelesses (Côtes de Beaune) (Premier Cru)
Aloxe-Corton (Premier Cru)	**Pommard (Premier Cru)**
Auxey-Duresses (Côtes de Beaune) (Premier Cru)	Puligny-Montrachet (Côtes de Beaune) (Premier Cru)
Beaune (Premier Cru)	St.-Aubin (Côtes de Beaune) (Premier Cru)
Blagny (Côtes de Beaune) (Premier Cru)	Santenay (Côtes de Beaune) (Premier Cru)
Chassagne-Montrachet (Côtes de Beaune) (Premier Cru)	Savigny (-Lès-Beaune) (Côtes de Beaune) (Premier Cru)
Ladoix (Côtes de Beaune) (Premier Cru)	**Volnay (Premier Cru)**
	(Le) Corton Grand Cru

Also try:

red Côte de Beaune red
Mercurey or red Rully

red Sancerre
red Alsace

BURGUNDY RED

Rest of Burgundy

These Pinot Noirs are fresh and fruity, with up-front red fruit: redcurrants, red cherries and raspberries. They are not as intense as other Burgundy Pinot Noirs, but are good value. These wines also go well with roast duck or beef. If you are looking for a curiosity, Irancy is red Chablis, and makes an unusual partner for fish.

Burgundy region

All red Burgundy is made from Pinot Noir, right? Wrong! Contrary to popular belief, basic red Burgundy can (and usually does) have a lot of Gamay in it. However, the best examples will say Pinot Noir on the label, and will be at least 85% pure. They are all easy drinking lunchtime wines, with up-front red fruit like red cherries, raspberries and cherries.

PRICE

	Bourgogne (Rouge) (village name)
	Bourgogne Passe-Tout-Grains
Irancy	Bourgogne Grand-Ordinaire
Givry (Premier Cru)	
Rully (Premier Cru)	
Mercurey (Premier Cru)	

Also try:
Touraine Pinot Noir
red Sancerre
red Alsace

Also try:
red Beaujolais
blended red Vin de Savoie

PINOT NOIR

Basic pink burgundy is dry and fruity, and good with a picnic on a hot day. Wines marked "Clairet" are darker pink, and are really light reds. Perhaps unsurprisingly given its reputation for reds, the Côte de Nuits produces the best pinks of Burgundy – particularly from Marsannay. They are dry, fruity and rich. Pinks from the Côte de Beaune are dry and fruity, and a little less rich than those from Côte de Nuits. Both make an excellent aperitif at the start of a meal where red Burgundy will be served.

Bourgogne (Rosé/Clairet) (village name)	Bourgogne (Clairet/Rosé) Hautes-Côtes de Beaune
Bourgogne (Clairet/Rosé) Hautes-Côtes de Nuits	Marsannay

Also try:
pink Sancerre (86)
pink Alsace (100)

Also try:
red Bourgogne Hautes-Côtes de Nuits

PINOT NOIR & GAMAY

Unlike the reds, adding Gamay makes a better wine than a pure Pinot Noir. They are dry and light, and are good as an aperitif.

Bourgogne Grand-Ordinaire
Bourgogne Passe-Tout-Grains

GAMAY

These wines are lovely if you can find them: light, fruity and fresh. They are super with a picnic or a cold lunch.

PRICE

Mâcon
Mâcon Supérieur
Beaujolais (village name)
Beaujolais Supérieur
Beaujolais-Villages

Also try:
pink Beaujolais
pink Côtes Roannaises
pink Touraine Gamay

Also try:
pink Côtes Roannaises
pink Touraine Gamay
pink Vin de Savoie Gamay

There are only two sparkling red appellations in France, one in Burgundy and one in the Loire. These wines are quite sweet so not to everybody's taste, but they can make a fun fizz for a change. Try as an aperitif with nibbles, and serve well chilled.

Pink Burgundy is dry and fruity, but is more rounded than Champagne. If you are looking for a good value alternative to pink Champagne, then pink Crémant d'Alsace is better.

Bourgogne Mousseux

Also try:
red Touraine Mousseux
Crémant de Bourgogne Blanc de Noirs

Crémant de Bourgogne

Also try:
pink Crémant d'Alsace
pink Crémant de Loire

PINOT BLANC & CHARDONNAY

PINOT NOIR & GAMAY

These wines are mainly Pinot Blanc, and have improved dramatically – no longer are they made from grapes that were not good enough to be made into still wines. They do not have the biting acidity that makes Champagne so successful, but they can be rich and toasty. A good aperitif wine, or a fine partner for egg dishes.

Blanc de noirs wines are white, but made from Burgundy's black grapes. These sparklers are dry, light and fresh and develop some biscuity character with age. They have less acidity than Champagne, but they still make a good aperitif.

PRICE

Crémant de Bourgogne
Crémant de Bourgogne Blanc de Blancs

Also try:
white Crémant de Loire
white Touraine Mousseux
Champagne Blanc de Blancs

Crémant de Bourgogne Blanc de Noirs

Also try:
Champagne Blanc de Noirs
pink Crémant de Bourgogne

Côte d'Or:

The producers listed here have excellent reputations. Whether white or red, Grand Cru or village wine, their wines should be delicious.

Dom **Amiot-Servelle**, Dom Robert **Ampeau** et Fils, Dom Marquis d'**Angerville**, Dom de l'**Arlot**, Dom Comte **Armand**, Dom Robert **Arnoux**, Dom **Bachelet**, Dom **Barthod-Noëllat**, Dom Jean-Claude **Belland**, Dom **Bertagna**, Dom **Bitouzet-Prieur**, Dom Simon **Bize** et Fils, Dom **Blain-Gagnard**, Dom Daniel **Bocquenot**, Dom Jean-Marc **Boillot**, Dom **Bonneau du Martray**, Dom Michel **Bouzereau**, Dom Alain **Burguet**, Dom **Capron-Manieux**, Dom Louis **Carillon** et Fils, Dom **Cathiard**, **Champy Père et Cie**, Dom **Chandon de Briailles**, Dom Philippe **Charlopin-Parizot**, Dom Jean **Chartron**, Dom du **Château de Meursault**, **Château de Monthélie**, Dom **Gérard Chavy** et Fils, Dom Michel **Chevillon**, Dom Robert **Chevillon**, Dom **Chopin-Groffier**, Dom Bruno **Clair**, Dom **Clavelier-Brosson**, Dom Georges **Clerget**, Dom du **Clos des Epeneaux**, Dom **Coche-Debord**, Dom **Coche-Dury**, Dom **Colin-Deleger**, Dom Jean-Jacques **Confuron**, Dom **Confuron-Cotétidot**, Dom de **Courcel**, Dom Pierre **Damoy**, Dom **Darviot-Perrin**, Dom Jean-Pierre **Diconne**, Dom Joseph **Drouhin**, Dom **Dubreuil-Fontaine**, Dom Claude **Dugat**, Dom **Dugat-Py**, Dom **Dujac**, Dom Maurice **Ecard**, Dom René **Engel**, Dom Frédérick **Esmonin**, Dom Michel **Esmonin**, Dom **Faiveley**, Dom **Fontaine-Gagnard**, Dom **Forey** Père et Fils, Dom Jean-Noël **Gagnard**, Dom **Gagnard-Delagrange**, Dom Michel **Gaunoux**, Dom **Geantet-Pansiot**, Dom Pierre **Gelin**, Dom Jacques **Germain**, Dom Vincent **Girardin**, Dom **Girard-Vollot**, Dom Henri **Gouges**, Dom Jean **Grivot**, Dom Robert **Groffier**, Dom A et F **Gros**, Dom Jean **Gros**, Dom Anne-François **Gros**, Dom **Harmand-Geoffrey**, Dom **Henri-Gouges**, **Hospices de Beaune**, Dom Alain **Hudelot-Noëllat**, Maison Louis **Jadot**, Dom **Jayer-Gilles**, Dom François **Jobard**, Dom Michel **Lafarge**, Dom des Comtes **Lafon**, Dom **Lamarche**, Dom des **Lambrays**, Dom Hubert **Lamy**, Dom Fernand **Lecheneaux** et Fils, Dom Philippe **Leclerc**, Dom **Leflaive**, Dom **Leroy**, Dom Hubert

Lignier, Dom Louis **Latour**, Dom **Machard de Gramont**, Dom Joseph et Pierre **Matrot**, Dom **Maume**, Dom **Méo-Camuzet**, Prince Florent de **Mérode**, Dom Alain **Michelot**, Dom **Michelot-Buisson**, Dom de **Monthélie-Douhairet**, Dom de **Montille**, Dom Bernard **Morey**, Dom Jean-Marc **Morey**, Dom Pierre **Morey**, Dom **Morey-Coffinet**, Dom Albert **Morot**, Dom Denis **Mortet**, Dom **Mugneret (-Gibourg)**, Dom Jacques-Frédéric **Mugnier**, Dom Philippe **Naddef**, Dom **Parent**, Dom Jean-Marc **Pavelot**, Dom **Perrot-Minot**, Dom Fernand **Pillot**, Dom **Ponsot**, Dom de la **Pousse d'Or**, Dom Jacques **Prieur**, Dom **Prieure Roch**, Dom le **Royer-Girardin**, Dom **Ramonet**, Dom **Remoriquet**, Dom Daniel **Rion** et Fils, Dom de la **Romanée-Conti** (DRC), Dom **Rossignol-Trapet**, Dom Joseph **Roty**, Dom **Rougeot**, Dom Emmanuel **Rouget**, Dom Guy **Roulot**, Dom Georges **Roumier**, Dom Armand **Rousseau**, Dom Étienne **Sauzet**, Dom Daniel **Senard**, Dom **Serafin** Père et Fils, Dom Jean **Tardy**, Dom Gérard **Thomas**, Dom **Thomas-Moillard**, Dom **Tollot-Beaut** et Fils, Dom Louis **Trapet**, Dom **Vachet-Rousseau**, Dom Comte Georges de **Vogüé** and Dom de la **Vougeraie**.

Beaujolais:
Dom **Aucoeur**, Jean **Benon**, Dom **Champagnon**, Michel **Chignard**, Dom du **Clos du Fief**, Jean-Marc **Desprès**, Georges **Duboeuf**, Hubert et Denise **Lapierre**, Marcel **Lapierre**, Alain **Passot**, Ch de **Raousset** and Ch **Thivin**.

Chablis:
Jean-Claude **Bessin**, Dom **Billaud-Simon**, La **Chablisienne**, Dom Jean **Collet**, Dom René et Vincent **Dauvissat (Camus)**, Jean-Paul & Benoît **Droin**, Dom Joseph **Drouhin**, Gérard **Duplessis**, Dom Jean **Durup**, Dom William **Fèvre**, Dom Michel **Laroche**, Dom de la **Maladière**, Dom Gilbert **Picq**, Dom François **Raveneau** and Dom Guy **Robin**.

(Abbreviations: Dom for Domaine, Ch for Château)

RHÔNE

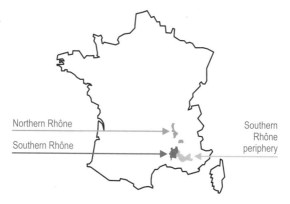

Northern Rhône

Southern Rhône

Southern Rhône periphery

The Rhône valley actually has two completely different wine producing districts, the Northern Rhône and the much larger Southern Rhône. The region produces some of the best wines of France, and thankfully these do not come with the very high prices that Bordeaux and Burgundy wines can command. Being further south than Bordeaux and Burgundy, the grapes ripen more easily and so the wines have a noticeably fruitier character.

The wines of the Northern Rhône are usually unblended single grape varieties, or a blend of just two grapes. The red wines are made from the Syrah grape – the same grape as Shiraz in Australia. These are dark, brooding and long-lived, full of spicy voilet flavours. The white wines are either made from a blend of Marsanne and Roussanne, or from Viognier. The Marsanne-Roussanne blends are dry and rich, and taste of dried fruit and hazelnuts – the best is white Hermitage which has the greatest aging potential of any dry white wine. The Viogniers are floral and fruity, and very aromatic.

In complete contrast to the North, the South and its periphery produces wines in mind-boggling blends of bizarre local grapes. The reds are full of peppery spice, and as a general rule Grenache is the main grape used – although in some cases like Châteauneuf-du-Pape up to thirteen different varieties are allowed. The white wines commonly use Grenache Blanc and Clairette in their blends, and are an exotic alternative to white Burgundy.

The Southern Rhône also produces sweet fortified wines. These are made in a similar way to Port, by adding brandy to stop fermentation before all the sugar from the grape juice is converted to alcohol. The result is a sweet and sticky wine with in-your-face fruit and higher than normal alcohol.

RHÔNE VINTAGES

Very good or great
Northern: 1982, 1983, 1985, 1988, 1989, 1990, 1995, 1999, 2000, 2003, 2004.
Southern: 1983, 1985, 1988, 1989, 1990, 1995, 1998, 2000, 2003, 2004.

Quite Good
Northern: 1980, 1986, 1987, 1991, 1996, 1997 1998, 2001.
Southern: 1980, 1981, 1982, 1986, 1993, 1994, 1996, 1999, 2001.

Mixed or poor
Northern: 1981, 1984, 1992, 1993, 1994, 2002.
Southern: 1984, 1987, 1991, 1992, 1997, 2002.

GRENACHE BLANC & CLAIRETTE

OFTEN BLENDED WITH VARIETIES SUCH AS BOURBOULENC, ROUSSANNE, VIOGNIER, UGNI BLANC, MARSANNE, VERMENTINO AND PICPOUL

These white wines from the Southern Rhône allow many different grapes into the blend. In general, though, they are rich, dry, crisp and fragrant, with a hint of exotic fruits. Their richness makes them a good partner for rich food, such as veal with wild mushrooms. If you appreciate offal like kidneys or liver, try these wines with them.

CLAIRETTE

OFTEN BLENDED WITH VARIETIES SUCH AS GRENACHE BLANC, ROUSSANNE, MARSANNE, BOURBOULENC, UGNI BLANC, VIOGNIER, PINOT BLANC, MAUZAC, AND PASCAL BLANC

These wines tend to be lighter, more neutral blends than those with a higher Grenache Blanc content, and they have a greater emphasis on freshness. Their simplicity means they go well with most chicken and white fish dishes, and are equally fine on their own with your feet up in front of the TV.

	Coteaux de Die
Côtes du Lubéron	Côtes du Ventoux
Coteaux du Tricastin	Coteaux de Pierrevert
Côtes du Vivarais	Côtes-du-Rhône
Lirac	Côtes-du-Rhône-Villages
Vacqueyras	
Châteauneuf-du-Pape	

Also try:
white Coteaux de Languedoc
white Corbières or Minervois
Montagny
white Graves
Entre-Deux-Mers

Also try:
white Mâcon
white Châteauneuf-du-Pape
Clairette de Languedoc
Cassis or Coteaux Varios

These white wines from the Northern Rhône are among the world's greatest white wines, with Hermitage in particular being able to age well. They are big and rich, with citrous notes and a hazelnut and dried apricot character. Try them with grilled white sea fish, like sea bass, halibut or turbot. Hermitage Vin de Paille is sweet, very rare, and is the only one outside Jura.

Viognier is a strange grape: it makes wines that smell like they are sweet, but are not. They are pale gold in colour, very fragrant with musky aromas of peach and lime blossom. They can be kept for a while, but are best young and fresh. Try on their own, or drink with crab bisque or pasta with olive oil and herbs. Château-Grillet is a tiny, single-producer appellation: Condrieu is often better quality and value.

Crozes-Hermitage

St.-Péray

St.-Joseph

Hermitage

Condrieu

Hermitage Vin de Paille

Château-Grillet

Also try:
white Pessac-Léognan
Entre-Deux Mers
Vin de Savoie Chignin-Bergeron
Jura Vins de Paille

Also try:
Alsace Riesling
Jurançon Sec
Tursan
Alsace Gewürztraminer

PRICE

ALIGOTÉ

CHARDONNAY

Châtillon-en-Diois Aligoté

Châtillon-en-Diois Chardonnay

Also try:
Bourgogne Aligoté

Also try:
white Bourgogne
Arbois Chardonnay

RHÔNE RED

SYRAH

Like their Aussie Shiraz cousins, these wines are big, dark and brooding. They have heaps of deep red fruit like morello cherries, blackcurrants and raspberries, with an aroma of violets, tar and smoke, and a dinstinctive spicy black peppercorn character. They can take on the heaviest meat dishes: game, beef and calves livers.

GRENACHE BLENDS

These wines are usually blends of many varieties, however Grenache is typically dominant. The Spanish name for Grenache is Garnacha, which is one of the principal grapes of Rioja. These wines are dark, plummy and spicy, with red berry fruit, cherries and blackerries. They are excellent with roast duck, roast beef and chicken liver dishes.

Brézème-Côtes-du-Rhône

Crozes-Hermitage | Côtes du Vivarais

St.-Joseph | Gigondas

Cornas

Côte Rôtie

Hermitage

Also try:
red Côtes du Frontonnais
red Côtes de Millau

Also try:
red Côtes-du-Rhône
Madiran

OFTEN BLENDED WITH VARIETIES SUCH AS CARIGNAN, PICPOUL NOIR, TERRET NOIR, PICARDAN, ROUSSANNE, MARSANNaE, BOURBOULENC, VIOGNIER, COUNOISE, MUSCARDIN, VACCARÈSE, PINOT BLANC, MAUZAC, PASCAL BLANC, UGNI BLANC, CALITOR, GAMAY AND CAMARÈSE

The red wines of the Southern Rhône characteristically allow a huge range of grapes into the blend. However, Grenache, Syrah, Cinsault and Mourvèdre are the dominant ones. The wines have a rich, full, dark and spicy character, with raspberry fruit and hints of leather. With age, they develop silkiness and cinnamon spice. They go well with meaty dishes such as beefburgers, dark meat casseroles, terrine, game, or duck.

Côtes du Ventoux	Coteaux du Tricastin
Côtes-du-Rhône	Coteaux de Pierrevert
Côtes-du-Rhône-Villages	Côtes du Lubéron
	Lirac
	Vacqueyras
	Châteauneuf-du-Pape

Also try:
red Gigondas
red Coteaux de Languedoc
Pic-St.-Loup

red Collioure
red Minervois

RHÔNE RED AND PINK

CINSAULT & GRENACHE

CINSAULT, GRENACHE, SYRAH & MOURVÈDRE

These pinks are fresh, ripe and fruity. They make great additions to picnics and al fresco meals.

These are probably the best pink wines in the world: full of fresh summer fruits but with a peppery character. They are rich enough to go well with river fish such as trout, crab, lobster and scallops.

Côtes du Vivarais
Vacqueyras
Gigondas

Côtes du Ventoux
Coteaux du Tricastin
Côtes du Lubéron
Coteaux de Pierrevert
Côtes-du-Rhône
Côtes-du-Rhône-Villages
Lirac

Tavel

Also try:
pink Côtes-du-Rhône
pink Béarn

Also try:
pink Costières de Nîmes
pink Collioure

GAMAY

GAMAY

Châtillon-en-Diois

Châtillon-en-Diois

Also try:
red Beaujolais

Also try:
pink Beaujolais

PRICE

GRENACHE BLANC & GRENACHE GRIS

MUSCAT

OFTEN BLENDED WITH VARIETIES SUCH AS PICPOUL, TERRET NOIR, PICARDAN, ROUSSANNE, VIOGNIER, COUNOISE, MUSCARDIN, VACCARÈSE, PINOT BLANC, MAUZAC, PASCAL BLANC, UGNI BLANC, CALITOR, GAMAY AND CAMARÈSE

MAY BE EITHER WHITE OR PINK, DEPENDING ON WHETHER IT IS MADE WITH MUSCAT BLANC À PETIT GRAINS OR MUSCAT ROSÉ À PETIT GRAINS

These sweet fortified wines can be red, white, pink or tawny. Rasteau should not be confused with village Côtes-du-Rhône Rasteau, a sub-appellation of Côtes-du-Rhône Villages. The reds can be a bit coarse and grippy, whereas the others are mellower. Generally, they have a grapey taste and a furry character like apricot skins. Better examples are made into "Rancio", meaning the barrels of maturing wine are left out in the sunshine for a couple of years at least, which results in a nutty, melted butter character. The reds make an interesting alternative to Port, and go well with harder cheeses. The other colours are good with sticky nutty puddings like pecan pie.

Muscat de Beaumes-de-Venise is the world's most elegant sweet fortified Muscat wine. It is made by adding grape spirit to semi-fermented wine, which stops fermentation while the wine still has much of its sugar. They are usually a golden apricot colour, although a few are pale gold, and have a distinctive grapey flavour. They have unusually low acidity for sweet wines, so they manage to go well with ice cream – avoid sorbets and fruity ice-creams, and go for the decadent creamy, nutty, sticky, toffee ones. Try with homemade brown bread ice cream for a perfect match.

PRICE

Muscat de Beaumes-de-Venise

Rasteau

Also try:
Banyuls
Maury

Also try:
Rivesaltes
Muscat de Frontignan
Muscat de Cap Corse
Alsace Muscat
Coteaux du Layon

CLAIRETTE

This wine is France's answer to Asti. Some people like it, but others think it is just fizzy, boring and neutral. Make sure you like it before serving it to your friends at a party.

Crémant de Die

Also try:
Blanquette de Limoux
white Crémant d'Alsace

MUSCAT

Unlike every other French sparkling wine, this is made using a single fermentation process, and ends up being decanted into a clean bottle for sale. These wines are sweet, and are deliciously fresh and fruity, with a ripe peach character. They go really well with fruit salads, particularly peaches with strawberries and raspberries.

Clairette de Die Méthode Dioise Ancestrale

Also try:
Champagne Demi-Sec
Alsace Muscat

RECOMMENDED PRODUCERS

Northern Rhône:
Thierry **Allemand**, Albert **Belle**, M **Chapoutier**, J-L **Chave**, Auguste **Clape**, Jean-Luc **Colombo**, Dom du **Colombier**, Yves **Cuilleron**, Pierre **Coursodon**, **Courbis**, **Delas**, Eric & Joël **Durand**, Bernard **Gripa**, E **Guigal**, Paul **Jaboulet Aîné**, Patrick **Lesec**, Jean **Lionnet**, Vignobles du **Monteillet**, Alain **Paret**, André **Perret**, Dom des **Remizières**, Marc **Sorrel**, Cave de **Tain l'Hermitage**, **Tardieu-Laurent** and Alain **Voge**.

Viognier (page 47):
All *Condrieu*.
Dom **Chèze**, Yves **Cuilleron**, **Delas**, Pierre **Dumazet**, Dom **Facchin**, Dom Matilde & Yves **Gangloff**, E **Guigal**, Paul **Jaboulet Aîné**, Alain **Paret**, André **Perret**, Robert **Niero**, Georges Vernay and François **Villard**.

These sparkling wines have a blossomy aroma, but can be fairly rustic and coarse for their price. Try them as an exotic curiosity, especially if the acidity in Champagne gives you stomach ache.

St.-Péray Mousseux

Also try:
white Gaillac Mousseux
Blanquette de Limoux

RECOMMENDED PRODUCERS

Southern Rhône:
Ch d'**Aquéria**, Ch/Coudoulet de **Beaucastel**, Dom de **Beaurenard**, Les **Cailloux**, M **Chapoutier**, Dom de la **Charbonnière**, Dom Gérard **Charvin**, **Clos de Caillou**, **Clos des Papes**, Ch **Fortia**, Ch de la **Gardine**, E **Guigal**, Dom de la **Janasse**, Dom de **Marcoux**, Ch **Mont-Redon**, Ch la **Nerthe**, Dom de **Pegaü**, Dom de **Piaugier**, Marcel **Richaud**, Ch **Rayas**, Ch de **St.-Cosme**, **Tardieu-Laurent**, Ch du **Trignan** and Dom de **Villeneuve**.

Fortified wines (page 51):
M *Muscat de Beaumes-de-Venise;* R *Rasteau.*
Dom **Coyeux** (M), Dom **Durban** (M), Dom des **Escaravailles** (R), Paul **Jaboulet Aîné** (M), Gabriel **Meffre** (M), Dom de la **Pigeade** (M), Ch **St.-Saveur** (M) and J **Vidal-Fleury** (M).

LOIRE

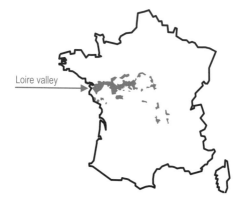

Loire valley

The Loire region is the largest wine-producing region in France, named after France's longest river. The wine producing districts along the length of this river are geographically spread out, and the wines and grape varieties used are diverse as a result. They do have one thing in common, though: the cool Northerly climate favours early-ripening grapes which make for crisply acidic wines.

The Loire has three distinct parts, each with their own choices of grapes and wine styles. Starting at the Atlantic Ocean, the first part of the Loire is the Pays Nantais which is influenced by the warming effects of the Atlantic Gulf Stream. The Pays Nantais is famous for its refreshing Muscadet wines, which are the classic companion to oysters.

The second part encompasses the wine producing districts of Anjou-Saumur and Touraine, which are dominated by Cabernet Franc reds and Chenin Blanc whites. Chenin

Blancs vary widely in style: they may be still or sparkling, dry or sweet. The sweeter styles such as the renowned Bonnezeaux and Coteaux du Layon are made only when noble rot affects the vines, which only happens in good years.

The third part of the Loire is the region between Orléans and Nevers, somewhat unimaginatively known as the Central Vineyards. This district is famous for its white wines made from Sauvignon Blanc, such as the mouth-wateringly crisp Sancerre. However, they also make reds from Pinot Noir which offer a worthwhile alternative to red Burgundy.

There are also many smaller wine-making districts further away from the river, and further upstream. These places are still make Loire wines, but they have little in common with those from the more famous districts. They are rarely exported, and many are classified as the inferior VDQS, rather than AC.

LOIRE VINTAGES

Very good or great
Sweet whites: 1985, 1988, 1989, 1990, 1994, 1995, 1996, 1997, 2001, 2002, 2004.
Reds: 1985, 1989, 1990, 1995, 1996, 1997, 2002, 2003

Quite Good
Sweet whites: 1986, 2003.
Reds: 1986, 1988, 1999, 2000, 2001, 2004.

Mixed or poor
Sweet whites: 1987, 1991, 1992, 1993, 1998, 1999, 2000.
Reds: 1987, 1991, 1992, 1993, 1994, 1998.

LOIRE WHITE

The Chenin Blancs of the Loire are amazingly versatile. They can be dry, sweet, still or sparkling, but it can be hard to tell from the label. Sometimes they will say "sec" for dry, "demi-sec" for off-dry, or either "doux" or "moelleux" for sweet. Otherwise, look at the bottle: dry wines are usually put in green bottles and sweet wines in clear. The dry wines are medium-bodied, firm, tangy and fruity with mineral and citrus notes. Savennières is very minerally, and can go with rich meats like goose, or rich fish like lobster or scallops. Other dry Chenin Blancs go wonderfully with lightly-flavoured seafish like grilled sole or plaice. Some wines below also come in sweeter versions, but should say "sec" or "demi-sec" on the label.

	Coteaux d'Ancenis Pineau de la Loire
Coteaux du Vendômois	Fiefs Vendéens
Touraine Chenin Blanc	Vins du Thouarsis

Coteaux du Loir	
Touraine-Amboise	Saumur (Sec/Doux)
Touraine-Mesland	Anjou (Sec/Doux)
Chinon	Anjou Coteaux de la Loire (Sec/Doux)
Vouvray (Sec/Demi-Sec/Doux)	Savennières
	Savennières Roche-aux-Moines
	Savennières Coulée-de-Serrant

Also try:

Côtes de Millau
Limoux

white Châteauneuf-du-Pape
Alsace Riesling

The sweet Chenin Blancs are among the best dessert wines in the world. They have aromas of apricots and pineapple, with the honeyed hallmarks of noble rot. These wines are wonderful with any fruit-and-cream pudding, like fruit cheescake or cherry pie with cream, but for a unique experience try with Chinese crispy Peking duck. Some wines below also come in dry versions.

These wines are some of the best examples of Sauvignon Blancs in the world. They are flinty and smell of cut grass, with a bit of gooseberry. They go with a wide range of foods: strong tasting fish like mackerel or trout; shellfish like crayfish or mussels; goat cheese, or camembert; chicken in creamy sauces; or artichokes dipped in melted butter.

	Haut-Poitou Sauvignon Blanc
	Coteaux du Giennois
Touraine Azay-le-Rideau (Sec/Doux)	Touraine Sauvignon Blanc
Quarts-de-Chaume	Cheverny
Coteaux du Layon	Menetou-Salon
Jasnières (Sec/Doux)	Quincy
Montlouis-sur-Loire (Sec/Doux/Moelleux)	Reuilly
Coteaux de l'Aubance	Sancerre
Coteaux de Saumur	Pouilly-Fumé
Bonnezeaux	

Also try:
Sauternes or Barsac
Muscat de Beaumes-de-Venise
sweet white Touraine Mousseux
Cabernet de Saumur

Also try:
St.-Bris
white Cheverny
Cour-Cheverny
Pouilly-sur-Loire

MELON DE BOURGOGNE

Muscadets are pale, neutral and aromatic, with high acidity. They can be very elegant, especially if they are "sur lie", which means they have spent a winter in contact with their yeast sediment to develop more flavour. They make a classic combination with oysters, green salad, or sea fish.

Muscadet

Muscadet
Coteaux de la Loire

Muscadet
Côtes de Grandlieu

Muscadet
de Sèvre-et-Maine

Also try:
Bourgogne Aligoté-Bouzeron
Clairette du Bellegarde
Gros Plant Nantais

CHASSELAS

Pouilly-sur-Loire wines are based on the Chasselas grape, which is normally for eating rather than making into wine. They are usually sharp and neutral in flavour with a subtle floral aroma, and can quickly taste tired. Try them if you are curious about what happens if someone makes wine from table grapes.

Pouilly-sur-Loire

Also try:
Alsace Chasselas
Crépy
white Quincy

PINOT BLANC

Dry, light and fruity, easy drinking aperitif wines

Haut-Poitou
Pinot Blanc

Also try:
Alsace Pinot Blanc

PINOT GRIS

These are lighter than Pinot Gris from Alsace, but still quite rich.

Vins de l'Orléanais
Auvernat Gris

Coteaux d'Ancenis Malvoisie

Also try:
Alsace Pinot Gris

Romorantin is a unique grape, grown almost nowhere else on Earth. It makes a wonderful aperitif for people who love Sauvignon Blanc but are looking for something with a twist. The nose is quite flowery, with a hint of grapefruit and the wine is dry, crisp and quite light-bodied.

Folle Blanche wines are usually neutral, thin and tart. Usually, they are destined to used to make brandy, because their neutral flavours and very high acidity actually make better brandy. Drink them if you want to know how undistilled Cognac would taste.

Valençay

Gros Plant (Nantais)

Cour-Cheverny

Also try:
white Sancerre
Cheverny
Clairette du Bellegarde

Also try:
Bourgogne Aligoté-Bouzeron
Clairette du Bellegarde
Muscadet de Sèvre-et-Maine

CHARDONNAY

SACY

Dry light and pleasant wines, and good value.

Sacy wines are crisp with high acidity, and a toasty full flavour.

Haut-Poitou Chardonnay

St.-Pourçain

Vins de l'Orléanais Auvernat Blanc

Côtes d'Auvergne

Also try:
white Bourgogne

Also try:
Alsace Pinot Blanc

LOIRE RED

Cabernet Franc is a Bordeaux grape that ripens early enough to thrive further North here in the Loire valley. The cool climate is evident in the taste of these wines: red cherry fruit and bell peppers, with aromas of violets, liquorice and pencil shavings. Drink them with chicken casseroles, goose (particularly rilette), or pork pies. Wines that just say "Cabernet" are usually blends of both Cabernet Franc and Cabernet Sauvignon.

Orléans-Cléry

Coteaux d'Ancenis Cabernet (Franc)

Valençay

Haut Poitou Cabernet Franc

Vins de l'Orléanais Cabernet Franc

Vins du Thouarsis

Touraine Cabernet (Franc)	St.-Nicolas-de-Bourgueil
Touraine-Mesland	Bourgueil
Touraine-Amboise	Anjou
Chinon	Saumur

Anjou-Villages (-Brissac)

Saumur-Champigny

Also try:

Touraine Cabernet Sauvignon
Touraine Cot
red Bordeaux

St.-Émilion
Premières Côtes de Blaye

Pinot Noir wines from the Loire have a more delicate flavour than Pinot Noirs from Burgundy. They have an aroma that is less like redcurrants and more like raspberries, perhaps with a slightly vegetal or beetrooty character. Delicious with slices of cold beef.

These wines are light, fresh and unpretentious, with masses of soft red fruits like strawberries and raspberries. They are good lunchtime wines to have with cold slices of cooked ham.

	Coteaux d'Ancenis Gamay
	Haut Poitou Gamay
Vins de l'Orléanais Pinot	Côtes d'Auvergne
Haut-Poitou Pinot Noir	Châteaumeillant
Coteaux du Giennois	Côtes du Forez

	Côtes Roannaises
Touraine Pinot Noir	Anjou Gamay
Reuilly	Touraine Gamay
Menetou-Salon	Cheverny

Sancerre

Also try:
Irancy
red Alsace
Bourgogne Rouge

Also try:
red Beaujolais
Bourgogne Rouge

PINEAU D'AUNIS

Another unique Loire grape, Pineau d'Aunis produces wines with a lively, peppery character.

Coteaux du Vendômois

Touraine
Pineau d'Aunis

Coteaux du Loir

Also try:
Touraine Cot
red St.-Joseph

MALBEC

These wines are deeply coloured and tannic, but are lighter in style than other Malbecs.

Haut Poitou
Cot

Touraine
Cot

Also try:
Cahors
red Cabardès

CABERNET SAUVIGNON

Late-ripening Cabernet Sauvignon does not always ripen well this far North, so it is usually blended with Cabernet Franc.

Coteaux d'Ancenis
Cabernet Sauvignon

Haut Poitou
Cabernet Sauvignon

Touraine
Cabernet Sauvignon

Also try:
red Bordeaux

PINOT MEUNIER

Pinot Meunier is more commonly used as one of the blending grapes in Champagne, but here it produces wines with a dark mushroomy character.

Touraine
Pinot Meunier

Also try:
Touraine Pinot Noir

PRICE

GAMAY & PINOT NOIR

Fiefs Vendéens

St.-Pourçain

MERLOT

Haut Poitou Merlot

PRICE

These pink Cabernet Freanc wines are a wonderful coral pink, and are dry fruity and refreshing with a smooth raspberry, strawberry and blackberry character. They have enough backbone to go with food, and are delicious with artichokes.

The pink Cabernet Francs from Anjou and Saumur tend to be made off-dry to medium sweet. Like drier versions, thay have full-on fruit. They are delicious as an aperitif, or a picnic wine.

| Coteaux d'Ancenis
Cabernet (Franc) |
| Valençay |
| Haut Poitou
Cabernet Franc |
| Vins de l'Orléanais
Cabernet Franc |
| Vins du Thouarsis |
| Rosé de Loire |

Touraine Cabernet (Franc)	Cabernet d'Anjou
Touraine-Mesland	Cabernet de Saumur
Touraine-Amboise	
Chinon	
Bourgueil	
St.-Nicolas-de-Bourgueil	

Also try:
Bordeaux Rosé
pink Buzet
Tavel

Also try:
Quarts-de-Chaume
pink Côtes de Provence

PINOT NOIR

GAMAY

These pink Pinot Noirs are fantastic: salmon pink in colour, fragrant and citrus with strawberry and raspberry fuit. If you like Pinot Noir, you must try these al fresco on a summer afternoon. They are also particularly good as an aperitif before serving a red Pinot Noir (either Loire or Burgundy) with the meal.

These are simple, dry, light-bodied, crisp, fresh and unpretentious pink wines. They have an appealingly grapey, strawberry and raspberry aroma, and make good picnic wines.

	Coteaux d'Ancenis Gamay
	Haut Poitou Gamay
Vins de l'Orléanais Pinot	Côtes d'Auvergne
Haut-Poitou Pinot Noir	Châteaumeillant
Coteaux du Giennois	Côtes du Forez
Menetou-Salon	Côtes Roannaises
	Touraine Gamay
	Touraine Azay-le-Rideau
	Cheverny

Sancerre

Also try:
Bourgogne Rosé
pink Alsace
pink Côtes du Jura

Also try:
pink Mâcon Supérieur
pink Beaujolais
pink Vin de Savoie
pink Côtes de Millau

PINOT GRIS

Since Pinot Gris is not a black grape, these wines are very pale pink, light-bodied and very dry. As they are the only pink wines made from this grape, it is worth comparing them to the full-on flavours achieved in an Alsace Pinot Gris – it is amazing how such different wines can be produced from the same grape.

Reuilly

Also try:
Lorraine Vin Gris
Bourgogne Rosé
pink Beaujolais
Alsace Tokay Pinot Gris

GROLLEAU

Grolleau is one of those grapes that has few distinguishing features, and is usually only used in a blend. Here it produces fresh and fruity wines that are a little sweet. Not to be taken too seriously, or drunk later than the spring after the vintage.

Rosé d'Anjou

Also try:
Quarts-de-Chaume
pink Côtes de Provence

PRICE

CABERNET SAUVIGNON

Coteaux d'Ancenis Cabernet Sauvignon

Haut Poitou Cabernet Sauvignon

Touraine Cabernet Sauvignon

PINOT D'AUNIS

Coteaux du Vendômois

Touraine Pineau d'Aunis

Coteaux du Loir

PRICE

GAMAY & PINOT NOIR

Fiefs Vendéens

St.-Pourçain

LOIRE SPARKLING WHITE

These white sparkling wines can be made either dry (brut), off-dry (sec), semi-sweet (demi-sec) or sweet (moelleux), and are either fully sparkling (mousseux) or semi-sparkling (pétillant). The Chenin Blanc is often blended with other varieties. They tend not to have the biting acidity of Champagne, but ironically, poor vintages help to boost the acidity which gives these sparklers a bit more backbone. Just pop the cork in good company and enjoy.

Saumur (Mousseux)	Montlouis-sur-Loire Mousseux/Pétillant
Saumur Pétillant	Anjou Mousseux
	Anjou Pétillant
Crémant de Loire	Touraine Mousseux/Pétillant
	Vouvray Mousseux/Pétillant

For drier styles, **Also try:**
white Crémant de Bourgogne
Champagne Brut

For sweeter styles, **Also try:**
Champagne Demi-Sec

RECOMMENDED PRODUCERS

Pays Nantais (pages 58-59):
For Muscadet or Gros Plant.
Guy **Bossard**, **Chasseloir**, **Coing de St.-Fiacre**, **Guindon**, Dom de la **Haute Févrie** and Louis **Métaireau**.

Sweet Chenin Blanc (page 57)
Dom **Alex Mathur**, Dom de **Bablut**, Patrick **Baudoin**, Dom des **Baumard**, Ch de **Bellerive**, François **Chidane**, Philippe **Delesvaux**, Ch de **Fesles**, Dom des **Forges**, Richard **Leroy**, Dom de **Montgilet**, Dominique **Moyer**, Dom **Ogereau**, Dom du **Petit Val**, Jo **Pithon**, Dom **Richou** and Dom de la **Taille au Loups**.

LOIRE SPARKLING RED AND PINK

Sparkling red wine is a bit of an oddity. These are light-bodied, fruity and refreshing, and must be served cold. They are made in tiny quantities, so if you can find them you should definitely try them.

Pink sparklers are very successful in the Loire. These wines are light-bodied, coral pink and definitely quaffable. They are made in a range of styles from dry to sweet, sparkling or semi-sparkling.

Saumur Mousseux

Anjou Mousseux

Rosé d'Anjou Pétillant/ Anjou (Rosé) Pétillant

Touraine Mousseux

Touraine Pétillant

Crémant de Loire

Touraine Mousseux/Pétillant

Also try:
pink Touraine Mousseux
red Bourgogne Mousseux

Also try:
pink Crémant de Bourgogne
pink Champagne

RECOMMENDED PRODUCERS

Dry Chenin Blanc (page 56)
Dom des **Baumard**, Dom du **Closel**, Ch de **Chamboureau**, Dom aux **Moines** and Ch de la **Roche-aux-Moines**.

Cabernet Franc (page 60)
Dom **Filliatreau**, Ch de **Hureau**, René-Noël **Legrand**, Dom des **Rochelles**, Ch de **Villeneuve** and Ch **Yvonne**.

Central Vineyards:
Henri **Bourgeois**, Jean-Claude **Châtelain**, Pascal **Cotat**, Lucien **Crochet**, Didier **Dagueneau**, André **Dezat**, Claude **Lafond**, Dom **Mardon**, Alphonse **Mellot**, Vincent **Pinard**, Salice de **Quincy**, Jean-Michel **Sorbe** and Ch de **Tracy**.

ALSACE (& LORRAINE)

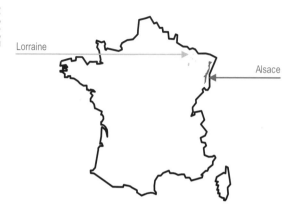

Lorraine

Alsace

Although Alsace is one of the most northerly wine making regions in the world, the Vosges mountains to the west shelter the district. The mountains make it unusually dry and sunny, and so suitable for growing grapes. The region is particularly famous for its white wines, sold in tall flute bottles, which have a unique and wonderful spicy character to them.

One fantastic thing about Alsace is that their labels are easy to read:

1 Most wines are made from a single grape variety, and that is clearly stated on the label.

2 There is only one appellation – Alsace AC – unlike the patchwork approach used everywhere else in France.

3 Most Alsace wines are dry, but sweeter wines are clearly marked "Vendanges Tardives" (late harvest) or "Sélection de Grains Nobles" (affected by noble rot).

4 The top fifty vineyard sites have been designated "Grand Cru" (great growth), and say so on the label.

The soils vary widely across the Alsace region, and consequently many different grape varieties are grown. However, the four "noble" grapes are Riesling, Gewürtztraminer, Pinot Gris (sometimes called Tokay Pinot Gris, or just Tokay), and Muscat.

Alsace-Lorraine has been under German control several times in history, and the German influence is apparent. Many of the grapes grown are German, not French. However Alsace wine is very different from German wines, many of which are much sweeter than their French counterparts.

Lorraine produces only tiny amounts from two varietal VDQS appellations, Moselle and Côtes de Toul. The nearly-pink "vin gris" is the speciality of this district.

ALSACE VINTAGES

Very good or great
Alsace: 1981, 1983, 1985, 1988, 1989, 1990, 1994, 1995, 1996, 1997, 2001.

Quite Good
Alsace: 1982, 1992, 1993, 1998, 1999 , 2000, 2002, 2003, 2004.

Mixed or poor
Alsace: 1980, 1984, 1986, 1987, 1991.

RIESLING

The Alsace wine producers regard Riesling as the highest of the four noble grapes. Rich, zesty and elegant, these wines can have a biting steeliness, and delicate aromas of citrus fruit, peaches and white flowers. With age, they develop a unique smell, which is often described as "petrol" – but that does not really do them justice. Dry versions are wonderful with strong-flavoured river fish like trout, or with chicken dishes.

GEWÜRZTRAMINER

Gewürztraminer is quite unlike any other grape grown in France: the wines are pungently aromatic and quite grapey when young, but develop spices like cloves and ground ginger, plus exuberant exotic fruit like lychees, citrus peel and grapefruit. They are full-bodied and characteristically have low acidity. Sweeter examples can be like gingerbread. Drink dry versions with Thai food, with avocado vinaigrette or with nutty cheese like gruyère. Try sweeter wines with foie gras.

Moselle Riesling	Moselle Gewürztraminer
Côtes de Toul Riesling	Côtes de Toul Gewürztraminer
(Vin d') Alsace Riesling	(Vin d') Alsace Gewürztraminer
Alsace Grand Cru Riesling	Alsace Grand Cru Gewürztraminer
Alsace Riesling Vendenge Tardive	Alsace Gewürztraminer Vendenge Tardive
Alsace Grand Cru Riesling Vendenge Tardive	Alsace Grand Cru Gewürztraminer Vendenge Tardive
Alsace Riesling Sélection de Grains Nobles	Alsace Gewürztraminer Sélection de Grains Nobles
Alsace Grand Cru Riesling Sélection de Grains Nobles	Alsace Grand Cru Gewürztraminer Sélection de Grains Nobles

Also try:
Condrieu
Alsace Sylvaner
For sweeter wines, also try:
Sauternes
Bonnezeaux

Also try:
blended Alsace
Condrieu
For sweeter wines, also try:
Sauternes
Jura Vins de Paille

Pinot Gris wines from Alsace are rich, smoky, tangy and spicy. This is the same grape as Pinot Grigio in Italy, but Alsatian wines pack a lot more punch. They are more acidic than Gewürztraminer, but less so than Riesling. As they age, they develop brazil nut and walnut aromas. Generally less dry than other Alsace wines, they go well with foie gras or white meat dishes like chicken casserole. The sweeter Sélection de Grains Nobles versions are awesome with crème brûlée.

Alsace Muscat is the only unfortified wine made from these grapes produced in France. Muscat grapes make the only wine that actually smells like grapes rather than some other type of fruit, although they can have delicate hints of rose petals, orange or peach. With age they develop hints of spice and liquorice. Dry versions go well with asparagus, and sweeter ones are fabulous with cheesecake.

Moselle Pinot Gris	
Côtes de Toul Pinot Gris	
(Vin d') Alsace (Tokay) Pinot Gris	(Vin d') Alsace Muscat
Alsace Grand Cru (Tokay) Pinot Gris	Alsace Grand Cru Muscat
Alsace (Tokay) Pinot Gris Vendenge Tardive	Alsace Muscat Vendenge Tardive
Alsace Grand Cru (Tokay) Pinot Gris Vendenge Tardive	Alsace Grand Cru Muscat Vendenge Tardive
Alsace (Tokay) Pinot Gris Sélection de Grains Nobles	Alsace Muscat Sélection de Grains Nobles
Alsace Grand Cru (Tokay) Pinot Gris Sélection de Grains Nobles	Alsace Grand Cru Muscat Sélection de Grains Nobles

Also try:
Alsace Pinot Blanc
Roussette de Savoie
For sweeter wines, also try:
Clairette du Languedoc

Also try:
Alsace Sylvaner
For sweeter wines, also try:
Muscat de Beaumes-de-Venise
Clairette de Die
Monbazillac

GEWÜRZTRAMINER, MUSCAT & RIESLING

Alsace is generally known for its "varietal" wines, which are made from a single grape variety. However, some of the very best Alsace wines are blends of the noble grapes. As they age their taste changes from grape to grape.

(Vin d') Alsace

Also try:
Alsace Gewürztraminer
Alsace Riesling
Alsace Muscat

SYLVANER, PINOT BLANC & CHASSELAS

Edelzwicker is dry, light and easy-drinking. These wines are generally clean, crisp and neutral, and would go well with cheese fondue.

Edelzwicker

Also try:
Alsace Sylvaner
Alsace Chasselas
Alsace Pinot Blanc

PINOT BLANC

Alsace Pinot Blancs are neutral, light and fruity wines – which makes this grape a popular component of Alsace Klevner and Edelzwicker blends. These wines are good with more delicate sea-fish like sole or plaice.

Moselle
Pinot Blanc

Côtes de Toul
Pinot Blanc

(Vin d') Alsace
Pinot Blanc

Also try:
Alsace Tokay Pinot Gris
Bourgogne Aligoté

AUXERROIS

Auxerrois is fatter than Pinot Blanc, and the wines have some of the spice for which Alsace is famous. There can also be buttery and rich honeyed notes in these low acid wines. They go well with French onion tart.

Moselle
Auxerrois

Côtes de Toul
Auxerrois

(Vin d') Alsace
Pinot Auxerrois/Gutedel

Also try:
Jurançon Sec
Alsace Tokay Pinot Gris

PRICE

CHASSELAS

Alsace Chasselas is quite sharp, floral and fairly uncomplicated. Try these wines if you are curious about what wine made from table grapes tastes like. Drink them as young as possible.

(Vin d') Alsace
Chasselas

Also try:
Pouilly-sur-Loire
Crépy
white Sancerre

SYLVANER

Alsace Sylvaner does not achieve the same intensity in Alsace as it manages to in Franken in Germany, but still has the characteristic earthiness. These wines are soft and simple, and make good aperitifs.

(Vin d') Alsace
Sylvaner

Also try:
Alsace Riesling
Bourgogne Aligoté

PINOT BLANC & AUXERROIS

PRICE

Alsace Pinot, or Alsace Klevner, is a little plumper than plain Pinot Blanc thanks to the addition of Auxerrois into the blend. Again these wines are good with grilled sea-fish, but would also make an attractive aperitif.

(Vin d') Alsace
Pinot/Klevner/Clevner

Also try:
Alsace Pinot Blanc
Alsace Pinot Auxerrois

SAVAGNIN ROSÉ

You would be forgiven for thinking Klevener de Heiligenstein used the same grapes as Alsace Klevner. In fact these delicate wines with a subtle spicy aroma are made from Savagnin Rosé, a refugee from Jura.

Klevener de Heiligenstein

Also try:
Côtes du Jura Savagnin
Jura Vins Jeunes

PRICE

CHARDONNAY

Moselle
Chardonnay

MÜLLER-THURGAU

Moselle
Müller-Thurgau

ALSACE RED & PINK

PINOT NOIR

PINOT NOIR & PINOT MEUNIER

Pinot Noir is a tricky grape to grow, and it struggles a bit this far North. Good examples have an honest, pure raspberry and red cherry fruit. They go well with chicken casseroles, roast pork, or soft cheeses.

Most red Moselle and Côtes de Toul are sold as varietal Pinot Noirs, however a few blended versions exist. The pure Pinot Noir versions are usually better.

| Moselle Pinot Noir |
| Côtes de Toul Pinot Noir |
| (Vin d') Alsace (Pinot Noir) |

| Moselle |
| Côtes de Toul |

Also try:
Irancy
red Sancerre

Also try:
red Coteaux ChampenoisTouraine Pinot Meunier

PINOT NOIR

GAMAY

MAY BE BLENDED WITH PINOT MEUNIER & PINOT NOIR

Pink Alsace Pinot Noirs are often much better than the reds. They are attractive, light-bodied and fragrant, with delicious strawberry, raspberry and cherry fruit. Like the reds, they go well with chicken casseroles or roast pork.

Vin gris is a speciality of the Lorraine district, and is not grey but very light pink. It is made exactly like white wine, only from black grapes. It is delicious drunk as young as possible.

| (Vin d') Alsace (Pinot Noir) |

| Côtes de Toul (Vin Gris) |

Also try:
Bourgogne Rosé
pink Sancerre

Also try:
pink Touraine Gamay
pink Beaujolais-Villages

PRICE

PINOT NOIR & CHARDONNAY

OFTEN BLENDED WITH PINOT BLANC & PINOT GRIS

Alsace sparkling white wines are generally very good. They make an interesting (and cheaper!) alternative to Champagne, and go well with egg dishes.

PINOT NOIR

Pink sparkling Alsace is usually even better than the white, and can be finer than pink Champagne. They are perfumed and delicious.

Crémant d'Alsace

Crémant d'Alsace

Also try:
Crémant de Die
white Crémant de Loire
Blanquette de Limoux

Also try:
pink Champagne
pink Crémant de Bourgogne
pink Crémant de Loire

RECOMMENDED PRODUCERS

White Alsace:
Barmès-Buecher, Dom Baumann-Zirgel, Jean Becker, Léon Beyer, Paul Blanck, Bott-Geyl, Albert Boxler, Ernest Burn, Dom Marcel Deiss, Dirler-Cadé, Pierre Frick, Hugel, Josmeyer, André Kientzler, Clement Klur, Marc Kreydenweiss, Seppi Landmann, François Lichtlé, Albert Mann, Dom Mittnacht Frères, René Muré, Dom Ostertag, Cave de Pfaffenheim, Cave de Ribeauvillé, Julien Rieffel, Rolly Gassmann, Schlumberger, Dom Schoffit, Bruno Sorg, Dom Marc Tempé, F E Trimbach, Cave de Turckheim, Weinbach, Wolfberger and Zind-Humbrecht

Red or pink Alsace:
Léon Heitzmann, Jean-Luc Mader and Dom François Otter.

Sparkling Alsace:
René Barth, Bernard Becht, Joseph Gruss, Klein-Brand, Cave de Pfaffenheim, Dom Rieflé and Wolfberger.

CHAMPAGNE

Champagne

Champagne is the world's most famous sparkling wine – and drinking it makes any event a celebration. Good champagne has a long-lasting stream of tiny bubbles, a wonderful balance between the sparkle and the underlying acidity of the wine, and a long-lingering taste – fruity and rich when young, biscuity and toasty after a few years. No other country can make a wine like it: partly because the region is so far North that the grapes really struggle to ripen every year, and partly because of the unique limestone and chalk soil.

Champagne is actually an official appellation, although it the only appellation that is allowed to drop the words "appellation contrôlée" on the label. The bubbles are made by making the wine go through a second fermentation in the bottle it will be sold in. This process also creates a yeast deposit which gives the wine more depth of flavour. This sediment is removed once fermentation and maturation is complete.

Most Champagnes are blends of Chardonnay, Pinot Noir and Pinot Meunier. They are blended across years to create non-vintage or "NV" wines with a consistent house style year after year. Single vintage Champagnes are usually more expensive, and most producers only declare a vintage in good years.

In addition, many producers make special editions called "prestige cuvées" – Dom Perignon from Moët & Chandon is probably the most famous, and I can vividly remember the 1990 Dom Perignon we drank to see in the new Millennium.

The region also produces still wines under the appellations of Coteaux Champenois and Rosé des Riceys. The conditions that make sparkling Champagne great also conspire to make Coteaux Champenois wines generally thin and expensive, however Rosé de Riceys wines can be some of the best pink wines in France.

CHAMPAGNE VINTAGES

Very good or great
Champagne: 1981, 1982, 1983, 1985, 1988, 1989, 1990, 1995, 1996, 2002, 2004.

Quite good
Champagne: 1986, 1991, 1992, 1993, 1997, 1998, 1999, 2000, 2001, 2003.

Mixed or poor – usually non vintage years
Champagne: 1980, 1984, 1987, 1994.

CHAMPAGNE STILL

CHARDONNAY, PINOT NOIR & PINOT MEUNIER

These white wines should be fresh, but can be thin. They are interesting historically because this is how Champagne used to taste before the method of making bubbles was developed.

Coteaux Champenois

Also try:
Muscadet
Alsace Klevner

PINOT MEUNIER, PINOT NOIR & CHARDONNAY

These red wines are the most promising Coteaux Champenois. In particular, those from the Bouzy or Aÿ sub-appellations in good years are distinctly Pinot Noir and can rival red Burgundy.

Coteaux Champenois

Also try:
red Alsace
red Bourgogne

PINOT MEUNIER, PINOT NOIR & CHARDONNAY

Made only in small quantities, these pink wines are very dry if you can find them.

Coteaux Champenois

Also try:
pink Alsace
pink Reuilly

PINOT NOIR

These wines can be some of the best pinks in France, and should be quite dark pink, herby and aromatic.

Rosé des Riceys

Also try:
pink Alsace
pink Bourgogne

PRICE

RECOMMENDED PRODUCERS

Billecart-Salmon, Bollinger, Deutz, Egly-Ouriet, Pierre **Gimmonet**, **Gosset**, Charles **Heidsieck**, **Jacquesson**, **Krug**, Larmandier-Bernier, **Laurent-Perrier**, Lilbert **Fils**, Serge **Mathieu**, Pierre **Moncuit**, Pol **Roger**, Louis **Roederer**, **Ruinart**, **Salon**, Jacques **Selosse**, **Taittinger**, Veuve **Clicquo**t and **Vilmart**.

Champagnes are normally a blend of both white and black grapes. Good Champagne has a fine sparkle, with a rich fruitiness and an aroma of brioches. When very old they can develop hints of coffee and coconut. Although often drunk as an aperitif, Champagne is excellent with many foods – even fish'n'chips!

Champagne
(Brut/Demi-Sec)

Also try:
pink Champagne
white Crémant de Loire

Blanc de Noirs Champagnes are white sparkling wines made from only the black grapes. They tend to be available only as the more expensive prestige cuvées. They age well, and develop a biscuity character. Like other Champagnes, these are marvellous with food, and cheese soufflé in particular.

Champagne
Blanc de Noirs

Also try:
Crémant de Bourgogne Blanc de Noirs
Champagne Blanc de Blancs

CHARDONNAY

Blanc de Blancs Champagnes are made from Chardonnay. These are the richest of all Champagnes and they will keep longer than any other sparkling wine. They have hints of walnuts and hazelnuts, and as they age they develop a toasty creaminess. Unusually for wine, they go well with egg dishes.

PRICE

Champagne
Blanc de Blancs

Also try:
white Crémant de Bourgogne
Champagne Blanc de Noirs

CHARDONNAY, PINOT NOIR & PINOT MEUNIER

Though they vary in depth of colour and richness, all pink Champagnes have a fine mousse of white bubbles. For the wine geeks, these are the only pink wines in Europe that are allowed to be made by blending white and red wines together. These make any party look decadent, but also go well with shellfish bisque.

Champagne Rosé

Also try:
pink Crémant d'Alsace
pink Crémant de Loire
white Champagne

JURA & SAVOIE

Jura

Savoie

The little-known Jura and Savoie wine-producing regions are located in the French Alps near the Swiss border, where the vines are often planted in treacherous places on the mountainsides. The most famous wines are "vin jaune" (yellow wine) and "vin de paille" (straw wine). They are both produced in Jura, and wines like them are found nowhere else on the planet.

Vin de paille is a very sweet white wine, made by a similar method to "passito" – a technique the Italians use to make their red Amarone wine. After harvesting, the grapes are laid out on straw mats (hence "paille" in the name) and left over winter. As the grapes slowly dry, the sugars in the juice concentrate. The raisin-like grapes are then pressed and the juice is fermented into wine, which is aged in oak casks for up to four years. These sweet dessert wines are golden in colour, and have a wonderfully complex, rich and nutty flavour.

The other famous wine of Jura is vin jaune, which is certainly a unique wine experience but some people find it a bit of an acquired taste. If you like fino sherry, you should definitely try this wine – vin jaune is like an unfortified version made from a different grape. It is made by sealing wine from the Savagnin grape in oak casks and leaving alone for six years. In that time, some of the wine slowly evaporates through the wood and two things happen: a layer of yeast grows on top of the wine, rather like it does on fino sherry; and the air gets in and slowly oxidises the wine. The results are extraordinarily rich and complex, with walnut, almond and dried apple aromas. Although these wines can be drunk as soon as they are released, they will last for over a century – as they age, they lose the in-your-face sherryness and develop great complexity.

Jura is also home to some unusual grapes: white wines are made from Savagnin and Chardonnay, and reds are made from Poulsard, Trousseau and Pinot Noir. They are frequently made from a single grape, which will be stated on the label. If no grape is mentioned, you are probably drinking a blend.

Savoie produces mainly sparkling and still white wines. Much of it is drunk locally as an après-ski aperitif, and so the wines are mostly easy-drinking and not very complex. Vin de Savoie from the Chignin-Bergeron sub-appellation is worth seeking out – it is made from the Rhône grape Roussanne.

CHARDONNAY & SAVAGNIN

SAVAGNIN

Jura's basic white wines are light, with aromas of alpine herbs and bracken, and are wonderful with a simple lunch of ham or pastrami and dill pickles. The vins de paille of Jura are some of the world's best sweet wines. The grapes are dried on straw mats to concentrate the juice before being pressed and made into wine. They are gold in colour, rich and complex, with nutty, raisiny aromas, candied fruit like figs and dates, and mangoes. Chill and serve with foie gras and blue cheeses, or chocolate desserts.

Jura's white wines are also produced as "varietal" Savagnin: light-bodied, with alpine herb aromas and some nuttiness. However, look for vin jaune. Drinking it can be an astonishing experience – vast, rich, dense and complex, sherry-like, with aromas of coffee, walnuts, almonds and dried apples. To really appreciate these wines, open them a couple of hours early and serve them at room temperature with the local cheese, compté, or some walnuts. They also work with mild curries, shellfish or foie gras.

Arbois	
Côtes du Jura	
L'Étoile	Arbois Savagnin
	Côtes du Jura Savagnin
	L'Étoile Savagnin
Vin de Paille d'Arbois/ Arbois Vin de Paille	Vin Jaune d'Arbois/ Arbois Vin Jaune
Côtes du Jura Vin de Paille	Côtes du Jura Vin Jaune
Vin de Paille de l'Étoile	Vin Jaune de l'Étoile/ L'Étoile Vin Jaune
	Château-Chalon

For basic wines, also try:
Beaujolais Blanc
For vins de paille, also try:
Jurançon

For basic wines, also try:
Klevener de Heiligenstein
For vins jaunes, also try:
Clairette du Languedoc Rancio

CHARDONNAY

Jura's white wines are also produced as "varietal" Chardonnay. These wines are light and uncomplicated with a herby character, and are good with cold meats and pickles.

Bugey

Arbois
Chardonnay

Côtes du Jura
Chardonnay

L'Étoile
Chardonnay

Also try:
blended white Côtes du Jura
Bourgogne Blanc

ALTESSE

Altesse wines from Savoie are fine, light and lemony-crisp with flowery aromas and a slight mineral tang. They go well with chicken dishes, raclette, and warm seafood salads.

Roussette du Bugey

Vin de Savoie

Roussette de Savoie

Seyssel

Also try:
Alsace Tokay Pinot Gris
Vin de Savoie Chignin-Bergeron

CHASSELAS

Chasselas is more usually a grape for eating, but here they are made into sharp, fruity, floral wines, with a touch of sparkle to lift them. Wines made for après-ski, they go with cheese fondues as their sharpness cuts through the melted cheese.

PRICE

Vin de Savoie
Marignan/Ripaille/Marin

Crépy

Also try:
Pouilly-sur-Loire
Alsace Chasselas

ROUSSANNE

The Roussanne grape from the Northern Rhône thrives in the Alps, and it makes some of the best white wines of Savoie. These are nicely rounded, with fragrances of almonds, hazelnuts, and dried apricots. They go well with river fish.

Vin de Savoie
(Chignin-) Bergeron

Also try:
Roussette de Savoie
white Hermitage

POULSARD, PINOT NOIR & TROUSSEAU

Although also available as pure "varietals" of Poulsard, Trousseau and Pinot Noir, these blended wines are more elegant. They can be floral and rich.

Arbois

Côtes du Jura

Also try:
Côtes du Jura Trousseau
blended red Vin de Savoie

POULSARD

The Poulsard grape makes wines that are very light in colour, tannin and body, with fruity red berry aromas. Great with chicken and other poultry, as well as cured meats.

Arbois
Poulsard

Côtes du Jura
Poulsard

Also try:
blended red Côtes du Jura
red Mâcon Supérieur

TROUSSEAU

Trousseau is the most tannic of Jura's indigenous black grapes. They have red and black berry fruit aromas, with hints of pepper spice. Over time, they develop a smell of autumn leaves. These go very well with game, venison or wild boar.

Arbois
Trousseau

Côtes du Jura
Trousseau

Also try:
blended red Côtes du Jura
Côtes du Jura Pinot Noir

GAMAY, MONDEUSE & PINOT NOIR

Most Savoie wine is white, not red. However there are some red wines made from Gamay, Mondeuse and Pinot Noir and are available as blends or varietals. The blends are usually better.

PRICE

Vin de Savoie

Also try:
Irancy
red Beaujolais

Savoie Gamays have this grape's characteristic fruity strawberry and raspberry aromas, but with an unusual peppery spice finish. Delicious with smoked ham or sausage.

These Mondeuse wines have a peppery forest fruit flavour of black berries. Try them with local French cheeses such as tomme and reblochon.

Bugey
Gamay

Bugey
Mondeuse

Vin de Savoie
Gamay

Vin de Savoie
Mondeuse

Also try:
red Beaujolais
blended red Vin de Savoie

Also try:
Vin de Savoie
red Cheverny

PINOT NOIR

These Pinot Noir wines are lighter than Burgundies, but have the characteristic raspberry and blackberry aromas. Splendid with sliced cold meats and salami.

Bugey
Pinot

Arbois
Pinot Noir

Vin de Savoie
Pinot Noir

Côtes du Jura
Pinot Noir

Also try:
blended red Côtes du Jura
Côtes du Jura Trousseau

Also try:
Irancy
blended red Vin de Savoie

POULSARD, PINOT NOIR & TROUSSEAU

These wines are firm and fragrant, and are produced in the same vin gris style of pink wines from Lorraine. They go well with light starters like artichokes.

Arbois

Côtes du Jura

Also try:
pink Vin de Savoie
blended red Côtes du Jura

GAMAY, MONDEUSE & PINOT NOIR

Pink wines of Savoie are fairly simple, light and fruity. Their dry to off-dry style makes a wonderful chilled aperitif.

Vin de Savoie

Also try:
pink Sancerre
pink Beajolais

GAMAY

Light, refreshing and dry, a good aperitif wine.

Bugey
Gamay

Also try:
pink Touraine Gamay

MONDEUSE

Light, refreshing and dry, a good aperitif wine.

Bugey
Mondeuse

Also try:
Rosé des Riceys

PRICE

PINOT NOIR

Light, refreshing and dry, a good aperitif wine.

Bugey
Pinot

Also try:
pink Sancerre

PRICE

These sparkling wines are generally uncomplicated, with an Alpine-clean and fresh fragrant character, and a light mousse.

White sparkling wines from Jura have finesse: they are fresh tasting, with small and long-lasting bubbles.

Vin de Savoie Mousseux/
Mousseux de Savoie

Vin de Savoie Pétillant/
Pétillant de Savoie

Vin de Savoie d'Ayze Mousseux/
Pétillant

Seyssel Mousseux

Arbois Mousseux

L'Étoile Mousseux

Côtes du Jura Mousseux /
Crémant du Jura

Also try:
Blanquette de Limoux
white Crémant d'Alsace

Also try:
Champagne Demi-Sec
Alsace Muscat

POULSARD

Rarely seen outside the region, pink Poulsard-based sparkling wines have a good reputation. If you like pink sparklers and are skiing in the Alps, you should look out for these wines.

PRICE

Bugey Cerdon

Arbois Mousseux Rosé

Also try:
pink Crémant de Loire

Also try:
pink Gaillac Mousseux

RECOMMENDED PRODUCERS

Jura (including Arbois, l'Étoile, Château-Chalon):
Ch d'**Arlay**, **Berthet-Bondet**, **Charbonnier**, **Durand-Perron**, **Labet**, Jean **Macle**, Dom de la **Pinte**, Jacques **Puffenay**, **Rolet**, André & Mireille **Tissot**

Savoie (including Bugey, Crépy, Seyssel):
Pierre **Boniface**, **Dupasquier**, André & Michel **Quénard**

SOUTH-WEST FRANCE

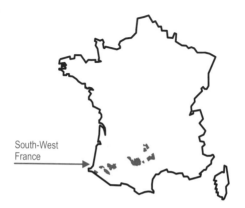

South-West
France

South-West France is a diverse wine-producing area between Bordeaux and Languedoc-Roussillon.

The wines from this region are made from an awesome variety of local grapes such as Manseng, Mauzac, Fer Baroque, Len de l'El and Négrette. The appellations themselves are not well known outside the region, so they tend to be good value. This combination of value and variety makes South-West France a fun place to explore new wines with strange names made from bizarre grapes.

In addition, these local grape varieties have been grown on this land since ancient times. The wines are liquid history, and drinking them can be like going back in time – especially when combined with the rich and diverse local food.

Tannat makes dark, meaty wines that have rich, chewy tannins. The wines are fruity, with an earthy spice finish. These wines go well with game birds like roast pigeon or pheasant.

Tursan

Côtes du St.-Mont		Béarn (-Bellocq)

Irouléguy		Madiran

Also try:
red Gaillac

Also try:
red Gigondas

FER

These can be fresh but a bit rough when young, they soften with age to become peppery and perfumed. Try with veal scallops.

Gaillac

Marcillac

Also try:
blended red Côtes du Jura
Côtes du Jura Trousseau

NÉGRETTE

These wines have a characteristic blackberry and violet aroma, and a touch of liquorice on the finish.

Vins de Lavilledieu

Côtes du Frontonnais (Fronton/Villaudric)

Also try:
Irancy
blended red Vin de Savoie

CABERNETS FRANC & SAUVIGNON, & MERLOT

Light-bodied, attractive, fruity and rustic. Try with beef sandwiches.

Vins d'Entraygues et du Fel

Vins d'Estaing

Also try:
red Bergerac

GAMAY & SYRAH

These wines are medium-bodied and fruity.

Côtes de Millau

Also try:
St.-Joseph

SOUTH-WEST FRANCE WHITE

GROS MANSENG, PETIT MANSENG, & COURBU

MAY BE BLENDED WITH OTHER VARIETIES SUCH AS LAUZET & CAMARALET

These grapes are virtually unique to this area. They are used to make both dry and sweet wines, and have a distinct tangy, spicy character. The dry wines are aromatic, with exotic fruit and grapefruit fragrances. The sweeter wines (Pacherenc du Vic-Bilh Moelleux and Doux, or Jurançon) have candied peel, pineapple, peach, and cinnamon aromas. Try the dry wines with sea fish, and the sweeter ones with grilled foie gras, roquefort cheese, or walnut tart.

BAROQUE

MAY BE BLENDED WITH GROS MANSENG, PETIT MANSENG & SAUVIGNON BLANC,

White Tursan is the only wine made from this unusual grape, and more modern examples can be full flavoured and aromatic. Many examples are still quite rustic, but the appellation is improving. They are good with grilled sea fish like herring.

Côtes du St.-Mont	
Irouléguy	
Béarn (-Bellocq)	Tursan
Jurançon Sec	
Pacherenc du Vic-Bilh	
Jurançon	

For dry wines, also try:
Condrieu
Alsace Auxerrois
For sweet wines, also try:
Jura Vins de Paille
Sauternes
Cadillac or Loupiac

Also try:
Condrieu
Coteaux du Languedoc La Clape

SOUTH-WEST FRANCE WHITE

MAY BE BLENDED WITH OTHER VARIETIES SUCH AS LEN DE L'EL, SÉMILLON & MUSCADELLE

This region is gaining the confidence to blend in more of its wierdly-named but more interesting indigenous grapes like Len de l'El, Mauzac and Ondenc. The dry wines are fresh, crisp and fragrantly appley, and go well with fish. Gaillac Doux is a sweet version wine which is rich, with honey and ripe peach aromas. Like other sweet wines, these go well with foie gras and roquefort cheese, and are also delicious with very ripe peaches or nectarines.

These wines are hard to find, but they are all dry, crisp and tangy, with an appley aroma. They would be good with a light lunch, and white meat dishes.

	Vins d'Entraygues et du Fel
Vins de Lavilledieu	Vins d'Estaing
Gaillac	Côtes de Millau
Gaillac Premier Côtes	
Gaillac Doux	

For dry wines, also try:
Montravel
white Graves
Bordeaux Blanc
For sweet wines, also try:
Monbazillac
Cadillac or Loupiac

Also try:
Gaillac
Vouvray Sec
Savennières
Limoux

TANNAT

Pink Tannat wines are fresh and simple with a delicate floral aroma. Try with fish dishes.

Tursan

Côtes du St.-Mont

Béarn (-Bellocq)

Irouléguy

Also try:
Tavel
pink Gigondas

pink Gaillac
red Béarn

FER

These pink wines are fresh, light, easy-to-drink and full of ripe fruit flavours. Lovely with tomato and basil salad.

Gaillac

Marcillac

Also try:
pink Bergerac

NÉGRETTE

These wines are very fruity, and make good wines to take on a picnic. A great match for spicy roast or fried fish, or fish soup.

Côtes du Frontonnais

Also try:
pink St.-Nicolas-de-Bourgueil

CABERNETS FRANC & SAUVIGNON, & MERLOT

These are light, fresh and pleasant to drink as an aperitif.

Vins d'Entraygues et du Fel

Vins d'Estaing

Also try:
Bordeaux Rosé

GAMAY & SYRAH

These are fresh and fruity and should be drunk very young.

Côtes de Millau

Also try:
pink Beaujolais

PRICE

These sparkling wines are some of the most interesting sparkling wines in France. Many of them are sweet, however whether they are dry or sweet, they are fresh, fragrant and appley.

Perhaps even better than the sparkling whites, these bright pinks are fresh and deliciously fruity.

Gaillac Mousseux Méthode Gaillaçoise	Gaillac Mousseux Méthode Gaillaçoise
Gaillac Mousseux Méthode Gaillaçoise Doux	Gaillac Mousseux Méthode Gaillaçoise Doux
Gaillac Mousseux Méthode Deuxième Fermentation	Gaillac Mousseux Méthode Deuxième Fermentation

For dry wines, also try:
Blanquette de Limoux
Crémant de Die
For sweeter wines, also try:
Champagne Demi-Sec
Blanquette Méthode Ancestrale

For dry wines, **Also try:**
Arbois Mousseux Rosé
For sweeter wines, also try:
pink Anjou Mousseux

RECOMMENDED PRODUCERS

B *Béarn*; F *Fronton*; G *Gaillac*; I *Irouléguy*; J *Jurançon*; M *Madiran*; P *Pacherenc du Vic-Bilh*; T *Tursan*.
Dom **Arretxea** (I), Ch d'**Aydie** (M), Ch/Baron de **Bachen** (T), Ch **Baudare** (F), Dom **Bellegarde** (J), Ch Bellevue la **Forêt** (F), Dom **Berthoumieu** (M), Ch **Bouscassé** (B, M), Dom **Bru-Baché** (J), Dom **Cauhapé** (J), Chapelle **Lenclos** (M, P), Clos **Lapeyre** (J), Clos **Uroulat** (J), Dom d'**Escausses** (G), Dom **Etxegaraya** (I), Herri **Mina** (I), Dom Labranche **Laffont** (M), Dom **Laffont** (M), Ch **Lafitte-Teston** (P, M), Ch **Montauriol** (F), Ch **Montus** (M), Dom **Mouréou** (M), Primo **Palatum** (J, M), Ch **Plaisance** (F), Ch le **Roc** (F), Ch de **Viella** (M)

(Abbreviations: Ch for Château, Dom for Domaine)

LANGUEDOC-ROUSSILLON

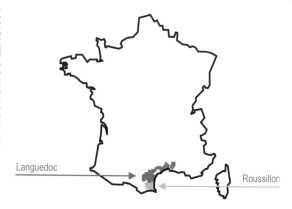

Languedoc

Roussillon

The Languedoc and Roussillon regions lie along France's Mediterranean coast. In the past, this region produced much of the European "wine lake" – lower quality wine that had no market, but was worth producing to collect government subsidies. Happily, there has been a shift to higher quality wines by many producers over the last two decades. But Languedoc-Roussillon still produces 40% of France's wines: 250 million cases a year, or nearly 900 Olympic-sized swimming pools.

The region is now a hot-bed for innovation in France's wine industry. Since none of the region's appellations command a high price, it has been a survival necessity. It is perhaps ironic that success holds back other regions from innovating – as they must continue to follow rigid appellation regulations in order to maintain their premium prices.

In Languedoc-Roussillon they are now making fruit-packed, early-drinking, New World styles wines from internationally recognised grapes.

Many of these new-style wines must be sold under the less restrictive Vins de Pays category, which allows producers to display the grape on the label and compete head-on with wines from places like Australia, New Zealand, South Africa and South America. Only a small proportion is sold under AC or VDQS appellations: over 85% is produced as Vins de Table or Vins de Pays. Some Vins de Pays wines, like Mas de Daumas Gassac produced under the classification Vin de Pays de l'Hérault, are classic fine wines – they just don't fit the French appellation system.

The region continues to make wines under traditional AC and VDQS appellations. Many of these have similarities with wines from the Southern Rhône. One appellation to watch out for is Coteaux du Languedoc, which has several sub-appellations with completely different rules. For example, the La Clape sub-appellation is a Bourboulenc dominated wine, and this grape manages to make refreshingly acidic white wines despite the high temperature in the region. Other sub-appellations include Picpoul-de-Pinet, which is made from the white Picpoul grape, and Pic-St.-Loup which is a red wine made from any proportion of Grenache, Syrah or Mourvèdre.

Some of the most interesting wines of this region are the sweet fortified wines. My personal favourite is Banyuls, which is a bit like Port, because this wine goes fantastically well with a really rich chocolate mousse.

GRENACHE BLANC & BOURBOULENC

MAY BE BLENDED WITH OTHER VARIETIES SUCH AS CLAIRETTE, MACABÉO, PICPOUL & UGNI BLANC

These are wines in transition. Traditionally, these have been just simple, dry and fruity. More and more, they are being developed to have more contemporary flavour. Cooler fermentation is making them fresher, and bringing forward the aromatic character of the grapes.

| Minervois | Costières de Nîmes |
| Corbières | Coteaux du Languedoc |

NB see below for Picpoul-de-Pinet or La Clape

Also try:
white Châteauneuf-du-Pape
white Cassis

Also try:
white Béarn
white Vin de Savoie

PICPOUL

Sometimes known affectionately as "pitbull", Picpoul-de-Pinet is an ancient grape which makes wines that are lively and fresh. Drink as young as possible.

Coteaux du Languedoc
Picpoul-de-Pinet

Also try:
Clairette de Bellegarde

BOURBOULENC

MAY BE BLENDED WITH MANY OTHER LOCAL VARIETIES

The way La Clape sounds in English, it is no wonder it hasn't been a marketing success outside France. Actually, these wines are some of the best whites in the Languedoc, and can be full-bodied and spicy.

Coteaux du Languedoc
La Clape

Also try:
white Tursan
Jurançon Sec

Clairette is not the most inspiring grape, but it achieves its full potential here in the Languedoc. These wines are simple, fruity, fresh and soft, with nuances of grapefruit and apple.

Wines marked Rancio have been sealed in their casks for three years and exposed to the sun, giving them a nutty, buttery character. They can also be fortified.

Clairette de Bellegarde

Clairette du Languedoc

Clairette du Languedoc
Rancio

For dry wines, also try:
white Côtes-du-Rhône
Alsace Tokay Pinot Gris

For Rancio wines, also try:
Jura Vins Jeunes
Rivesaltes Rancio

CHARDONNAY AND/OR CHENIN BLANC

MACABÉO & TOURBAT

Limoux has recently had its appellation rules changed to allow up to 85% Chardonnay or Chenin Blanc, and the results are a success: fresh, lemon-zesty and rich. Much more Chardonnay is produced than Chenin Blanc.

Roussillon makes much more (and much better) red wine than white. These wines can often lack the acidity necessary to make them refreshing and appealing – leaving them flabby. However, some fat and floral examples can be found.

Limoux

Côtes du Roussillon

Also try:
white Côtes de Beaune
white Côtes de Millau

Also try:
white Vin de Corse
white Côtes-du-Rhône

GRENACHE, SYRAH, MOURVÈDRE & LLADONER PELUT

MAY BE BLENDED WITH OTHER VARIETIES SUCH AS CARIGNAN & CINSAULT

These wines are full bodied, with honest up-front fruit, raspberry, blackberry and red cherry aromas, and hints of leather and pepper. They go well with dishes like chicken casserole. Their big fruit style makes them great wines for al fresco lunches in summertime.

Minervois (La Livinière)	St.-Chinian
Faugères	Coteaux du Languedoc

NB see below for Pic-St.-Loup

Also try:
red Côtes-du-Rhône
red Bandol

Also try:
red Les Baux de Provence
red Collioure

GRENACHE / SYRAH / MOURVÈDRE

MAY BE BLENDED WITH CARIGNAN AND CINSAULT

These wines have delicious dark cherry fruit, with spice and leather aromas. Pic-St.-Loup is giving Southern Rhône reds like Châteauneuf-du-Pape a run for their money. They are delicious with a steak, or cassoulet.

MERLOT / MALBEC / CINSAULT

MAY BE BLENDED WITH OTHER GRAPES LIKE SYRAH, GRENACHE

These wines are the Bordeaux blends of the South: less in-your-face fruit and spice, and more of the classic Bordeaux characters of elegant fruit, cigar-box and cedar. Great value alternatives to Bordeaux reds, they go well with beef or lamb dishes.

PRICE

Côtes de la Malapère

Costières de Nîmes

Cabardès / Côtes du Cabardès at de l'Orbiel

Coteaux du Languedoc
Pic-St.-Loup

Also try:
red Côtes-du-Rhône
red Collioure

Also try:
red Bandol
red Les Baux de Provence

MAY BE BLENDED WITH OTHER VARIETIES SUCH AS MOURVÈDRE, MACABÉO & CINSAULT

These are full-flavoured, rich fruity reds. They can have a herby character, and become spicy with age. They are delicious with chicken livers, cooked ham, or terrine.

Côtes du Roussillon

Côtes du Roussillon Villages

Fitou

Also try:
red Corbières
red Côtes de Provence

Also try:
red Collioure
red Bandol

GRENACHE & MOURVÈDRE

MAY BE BLENDED WITH CARIGNAN, SYRAH AND CINSAULT

Collioure is the Pan-Galactic Gargle Blaster of French wine, and a rival for some of the blockbusting Aussie reds. These wines are dark, concentrated, deep and powerful, with a distinctly spicy finish. They are effectively unfortified Banyuls, and are delicious with cassoulet and heavier meat dishes.

CARIGNAN & SYRAH

MAY BE BLENDED WITH OTHER LOCAL VARIETIES

Corbières is a huge appellation with really varied terrain and many blending options, so there is no dominant style. The wines should be full-bodied, with juicy, spicy cherry and raspberry fruit, with a hint of vanilla. A wine to enjoy with lamb chops or steak.

Corbières

Collioure

Also try:
red Côtes de Provence
red Gigondas

Also try:
red Côtes-du-Rhône
red Bandol

LANGUEDOC-ROUSSILLON PINK

CINSAULT, GRENACHE, SYRAH, MOURVÈDRE & LLADONER PELUT

MAY BE BLENDED WITH OTHER VARIETIES SUCH AS CARIGNAN

Like most other Languedoc pinks, these wines are dry, fragrant and floral, with a delicate ripe fruity character. Excellent match for pasta with tomato sauce.

Minervois (La Livinière)	St.-Chinian

Faugères	Coteaux du Languedoc

NB see below for Pic-St.-Loup

Also try:
red Côtes-du-Rhône
red Bandol

Also try:
red Les Baux de Provence
red Collioure

GRENACHE / SYRAH / MOURVÈDRE

MAY BE BLENDED WITH OTHER GRAPES LIKE CINSAULT

Like most other Languedoc pinks, these wines are dry, attractive, and have fruity and slightly floral aromas. Terrific with lasagna or spaghetti bolognese.

CINSAULT & GRENACHE

MAY BE BLENDED WITH OTHER GRAPES LIKE SYRAH, GRENACHE

These wines are mid pink and dry, full of ripe fruit flavours with a slightly fragrant floral character. They go well with mixed salads.

PRICE

	Côtes de la Malapère

Costières de Nîmes	Cabardès/Côtes du Cabardès at de l'Orbiel

Coteaux du Languedoc Pic-St.-Loup	

Also try:
pink Faugères
pink Bandol

Also try:
Bordeaux Rosé
pink Buzet

MAY BE BLENDED WITH OTHER VARIETIES SUCH AS MOURVÈDRE AND MACABÉO

These wines are attractively rose coloured, fragrant and floral, and they go well with pizza or mixed salads.

Côtes du Roussillon	Corbières

Also try:

red Corbières

red Côtes de Provence

red Collioure

red Bandol

CINSAULT, GRENACHE & MOURVÈDRE

MAY BE BLENDED WITH CARIGNAN AND SYRAH

Not very much Collioure pink is made, but those produced are ruby in colour and generously fresh, forward and dry. For a pink wine, these pack quite a punch, and can rival Tavel as the best pink wine in France. These wines are lovely with grilled vegetables or trout.

Collioure

Also try:

Tavel

pink Costières de Nîmes

LANGUEDOC-ROUSSILLON FORTIFIED

GRENACHE

These Grenache-based fortified wines are huge and complex. Banyuls is France's answer to Port, and has aromas of cocoa, coffee, preserved fruit and spice. Maury is more tangy and toasty, with hints of fig and tobacco. Both are excellent with chocolate desserts, and chocolate mousse in particular. Rivesaltes, however, comes in many styles: red, white, pink, or a sort of tawny-brown. The reds are soupy and tannic, with a chocolate and dark cherry character. These can age up to 40 years and should be served at room temperature. Other colours of Rivesaltes have a more raisiny, candied orange peel character, and are best served cold. Wines marked "Rancio" have been exposed in their barrels to heat and air, which gives them a distinctive nutty/melted butter smell.

Rivesaltes (Rancio)

Banyuls (Rancio)

Banyuls Grand Cru (Rancio)

Maury

Also try:
Rasteau

MUSCAT

These fortified Muscats are orangey-golden coloured wines with a sweet, light-but-rich, raisiny character. They actually smell of grapes, and have a wonderful delicate honeyed finish. They are fantastic served cold with rich cheesecakes.

PRICE

Muscat de Rivesaltes

(Muscat de/Vin de) Frontignan

Muscat de Lunel

Muscat de Mireval

Muscat de St.-Jean-de-Minervois

Also try:
Muscat de Beames-de-Venise
Muscat de Cap Corse

Blanquette is the local name for the appley Mauzac grape. Blanquette de Limoux is dry and rustic. Blanquette Méthode Ancestrale is a sweet curiosity, using the world's most ancient method of intentionally putting bubbles in wine, making it creamy and smooth with a toasty apple flavour. Both are aperitifs.

Crémant de Limoux is dry, and more refined than the Blanquette wines. It should be drunk as an aperitif.

Blanquette de Limoux

Blanquette Méthode Ancestrale

Crémant de Limoux

Also try:
Crémant de Die
Champagne Demi-Sec

For dry wines, also try:
white Crémant d'Alsace

RECOMMENDED PRODUCERS

B *Banyuls*; C *Corbières*; Ca *Cabardès*; Col *Collioure*; Cos *Cos. de Nîmes*; CL *Cot. du Languedoc*; F *Faugères*; M *Minervois*; Ma *Maury*; Mus *Muscat*; R *Côtes du Roussillon*; Riv *Rivesaltes*; S *St.-Chinian*; V *Vin de Pays*.

Ch **Aiguilloux** (C), Dom des **Aires Hautes** (M), Dom **Alquier** (F), Dom **Borie de Maurel** (M), Dom de **Cabrol** (Ca), Dom **Canet Valette** (S), Dom la **Cazenove** (R), Dom **Cazes Frères** (R, Riv, Mus), Dom des **Chênes** (R, Riv, Mus), **Clos Centeilles** (M), Dom du **Clos des Fées** (R), Ch **Coupe-Roses** (M), Ch des **Estanilles** (F), Dom **Ferrer Ribière** (R); Dom **Font Caude** (CL, V), Dom **Foulaquier** (CL), Dom **Gauby** (R), Ch **Grande Cassagne** (Cos), Dom de la **Grange des Pères** (V), Ch **Grès St.-Paul** (CL, M), Dom du **Mas Blanc** (Col, B), **Mas Jullien** (CL), Ch de **Lastours** (C), Dom **Lhéritier**, Dom **Marcevol** (R), **Mas Amiel** (Ma, Riv, Mus) **Mas de Daumas-Gassac** (V), Ch de la **Négly** (CL), Ch **Pech Redon** (CL), Dom de la **Rectoire** (Col, B); Ch **Rouquette-sur-Mer** (CL), **Tardieu-Laurent** (M, C, Cos), Dom la **Tour Vielle** (Col).

PROVENCE

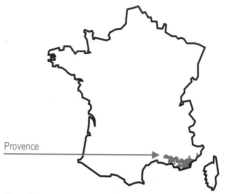

Provence

The climate in Provence is classically sunny and Mediterranean. It is famous as a holiday destination for Europe's mega-rich.

The most famous wines from Provence are pink. However, it is so hot that the grapes get very ripe, and making wines with enough refreshing acidity can be a challenge unless the grapes are grown at some altitude. Some pink wines may taste flabby as a result, and also tend to be expensive.

The reds are more promising, and these are full bodied and spicy. They are heavily influenced by the nearby Southern Rhône grapes like Carignan, Grenache, Cinsault and Mourvèdre.

The whites have high proportions of Ugni Blanc. This is the same variety as Trebbiano in Italy, but is rather dull and boring wine. The rest of France saw sense and used this grape for a higher purpose: distilling it into Cognac and Armagnac.

GRENACHE & CARIGNAN

These wines have big spicy blackcurrant and dark cherry characters. They are wonderful with rustic salami, or with lamb dishes.

Côtes de Provence

Coteaux d'Aix-en-Provence

Also try:
red Les Baux de Provence
red Corbières
Fitou

GRENACHE & MOURVÈDRE

These wines are deep and dark, full of flavours of plums and cherries, sometimes with a hint of chocolate. Their richness rivals Rhône reds. Try with strongly-flavoured meaty meals like peppered steak or calf's liver.

Coteaux Varios

Cassis

Les Baux de Provence

Palette

Also try:
red Les Baux de Provence
red Corbières
Fitou

BRAQUET, FUELLA & CINSAULT

For us wine geeks, Braquet is the same grape as Italy's Brachetto. These wines are extremely fragrant, considering how far South they are made, and have a full-bodied earthy character.

PRICE

(Vin de) Bellet

Also try:
red Cabardès
Cahors
Madiran

MOURVÈDRE

Mourvèdre is a deliciously intense, spicy grape and this is the only wine in France that leads with it. The wines are almost purple-black, with plenty of plummy fruit and a complex aroma of blackcurrants, cinnamon, violets and vanilla.

(Vin de) Bandol

Also try:
red Collioure
red Coteaux du Languedoc Pic-St.-Loup

CINSAULT, GRENACHE & MOURVÈDRE

PROVENCE PINK

Like their red counterparts, these pinks compete with the best of the Rhône. They are coral coloured, dry and refreshing, with a rich aroma of redcurrants and a peppery finish. Nearly all of Provence's best pink wines are produced under these appellations. These are generally smaller than other appellations in this region, and can be planted at some altitude above sea-level so that the grapes are kept cooler and do not over-ripen.

Coteaux Varios

Cassis

(Vin de) Bandol

Palette

Les Baux de Provence

Also try:
pink Collioure
Tavel
pink Costières de Nîmes

Also try:
pink Coteaux d'Aix-en-Provence
pink Cabardès

CINSAULT, BRAQUET & FUELLA

The pink wines of Bellet use the same varieties as the reds. They make dry, full-bodied pink wines with a fresh and floral aroma.

CINSAULT, GRENACHE & CARIGNAN

One in two bottles of French pink wine are Côtes de Provence. With production this large, wines can vary from intense and fruity, to light and peppery.

PRICE

Côtes de Provence

Coteaux d'Aix-en-Provence

(Vin de) Bellet

Also try:
pink Cabardès
pink Béarn
Tavel

Also try:
pink Côtes du Roussillon
pink Corbières
pink Cabardès

High temperatures make Provence a difficult place to make really interesting white wine, since fully ripe grapes lack the acidity to make the wines refreshing. Ugni Blanc, which is the same grape as Italy's Trebbiano, is naturally high in acidity but quite neutral (qualities that elsewhere in France make this grape a primary ingredient in Armagnac and Cognac). These wines are dry and fruity, with a soft aromatic quality that is sometimes quite herby. Some very good examples are made, particularly from grapes grown at higher altitudes. Cassis and Bellet are often the best, and these go well with local fish dishes such as sea bass with fennel, or octopus provençale.

Côtes de Provence	
Coteaux d'Aix-en-Provence	Coteaux Varios
Palette	(Vin de) Bandol
Cassis	(Vin de) Bellet

Also try:
white Côtes-du-Rhône
white Corbières or Minervois

Also try:
white Coteaux du Languedoc
white Vin de Corse

RECOMMENDED PRODUCERS

d'A *Coteaux d'Aix-en-Provence;* B *Bandol;* Be *Bellet;* C *Côtes de Provence;* CV *Coteaux Varios;* P *Pallette;* V *Vin de Pays.*
Dom des **Béates** (d'A), Ch de **Bellet** (Be), Dom **Bunan** (B), Ch de **Calissanne** (d'A), **Commanderie de Peyrassol** (C), Dom de la **Courtade** (C), Jean-Pierre **Gaussen** (B), Dom de **Gros' Noré** (B), Dom **Lafran-Veyrolles** (B), Dom de **Pibarnon** (B), Ch. **Pradeaux** (B), Dom **Richeaume** (C), Dom de **Roquefort** (C), Dom de **St.-Jean de Villecroze** (CV), Ch **Ste.-Roseline** (C), Ch **Simone** (P), Dom la **Suffrène** (B), Dom **Tempier** (B), Dom de la **Tour du Bon** (B), Dom de **Trévallon** (V).

CORSICA

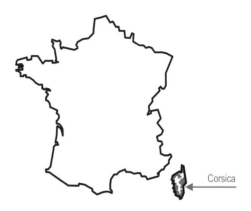

Corsica

Corsica is closer to Italy, both physically and culturally, than to France. As a result, the Corsicans use some Italian grapes, such as the Sardinian grape Vermentino for white wines, and Tuscan grape Sangiovese is apparently descended from the Corsican Nielluccio.

The islanders are independent and insular, and their wines reflect this. The land is very varied, and vines grow everywhere. However, only 5% of wine produced here is classified as appellation contrôlée, and those tend to be local in style and rarely exported.

The Corsicans also make a sublime fortified sweet Muscat, Muscat du Cap Corse, which is probably the best fortified Muscat produced anywhere.

These wines are full of rounded forward fruit, with a peppery finish. Almost unobtainable outside Corsica.

Nielluccio is the local name for Italy's Sangiovese, the primary grape in Chianti. Patrimonio can be very good, with a herby, meaty character and often a very peppery finish.

(Vin de) Corse

Ajaccio
Also try:
red Bellet

Patrimonio
Also try:
red Ajaccio

SCIACARELLO & NIELLUCCIO

NIELLUCCIO

These pinks are light coloured and peppery. They are easy drinking wines to relax with.

These wines are an attractive coral-pink and fine tasting, and are usually good value for their quality.

(Vin de) Corse

Ajaccio

Also try:
pink Patrimonio

Patrimonio

Also try:
pink Bandol

VERMENTINO & UGNI BLANC

MUSCAT

PRICE

These whites are dry, light and fruity, and are good with fish.

One of the world's best Muscats. Aromas of grapes, honey, cloves and liquorice. Delicious with nutty/toffee ice creams.

(Vin de) Corse

Ajaccio

Patrimonio

Also try:
white Côtes du Roussillon

Muscat du Cap Corse

Also try:
Muscat de Beaumes-de-Venise

INDEX

Abbreviations used:
R – red
W – white
P – pink
SR – sparkling red
SW – sparkling white
SP – sparkling pink
F – fortified with spirit

For those wines that are worth cellaring, this index also includes a recommended time range if this is greater than 2 years.

A

AC, see Appellation Contrôlée
Ajaccio, AC, Corsica: W p109, R p109 and P p109
Aligoté, white grape, p34 p47 p84
Aloxe-Corton, AC, Burgundy (Côte de Beaune): W p33 (4-8 years) and R p38 (4-15 years)
Alsace, AC: W p70-73 (blended Alsace 3-20 years, Riesling 4-20 years, Pinot Gris 5-10 years, Gewürztraminer 3-10 years, vendange tardives 5-20 years, sélection de grains nobles 5-30 years), R p74 and P p74
Altesse, white grape, p83 p87
Anjou, AC, Loire: W p56 and R p60
Anjou Coteaux de la Loire, AC: W p56
Anjou Gamay, AC, Loire: R p61
Anjou Mousseux, AC, Loire: SW p66 and SP p67
Anjou Pétillant, AC, Loire: SW p66 and SP p67
Anjou Rosé Pétillant, see P Anjou Pétillant
Anjou-Villages, AC, Loire: R p60 (2-6 years)

Appellation (d'Origine) Contrôlée, sometimes referred to as AC or AOC, the highest level in the French wine classification system, above Vins Délimités de Qualité Supérieure
Arbois, AC, Jura: W p82-83 (vin de paille 10-50 years, vin jeune 10-100 years), R p84-85 (2-8 years, except Trousseau 3-12 years) and P p86
Arbois Mousseux, AC, Jura: SW p87 and SP p87
Arbois Mousseux Rosé, see P Arbois Mousseux
Auxerrois, white grape, p72 p73
Auxey-Duresses, AC, Burgundy (Côte de Beaune): W p32 (3-10 years) and R p38 (6-15 years)

B

Bandol, AC, Provence: W p107, R p105 (3-12 years) and P p106
Banyuls, AC, Roussillon: F p102 (10-20 years)
Banyuls Grand Cru, AC, Roussillon: F p102 (10-20 years)
Baroque, white grape, p90
Barsac, AC, Bordeaux (Left Bank): W p17 (6-25 years)
Bâtard-Montrachet, AC and Grand Cru, Burgundy (Côte de Beaune): W p33 (8-20 years)
Les Baux de Provence, AC: R p105 (4-10 years) and P p106
Béarn, AC, SW France: W p90, R p89 (1-4 years) and P p92
Béarn-Bellocq, see Béarn
Beaujolais, AC: W p34, R p35 and P p40
Beaujolais Blanc, see W Beaujolais
Beaujolais Nouveau, see Beaujolais
Beaujolais Primeur, see Beaujolais
Beaujolais Supérieur, AC: W p34, R p35 (3-8 years) and P p40

Beaujolais-Villages, AC, Beaujolais: W p34, R p35 (3-8 years) and P p40

Beaune, AC, Burgundy (Côte de Beaune): W p32 (3-12 years) and R p38 (6-20 years)

Bellet, AC, Provence: W p107, R p105 (4-10 years) and P p106

Bergerac, AC, Bordeaux satellites: W p16, R p20 (2-8 years) and P p21

Bergerac Moelleux, see semi-sweet W Bergerac

Bergerac Sec, see dry W Bergerac

Bergeron, sub-appellation of Vin de Savoie, for W varietal Roussanne

Bienvenues-Bâtard-Montrachet, AC and Grand Cru, Burgundy (Côte de Beaune): W p33 (8-20 years)

Blagny, AC, Burgundy (Côte de Beaune): R p38 (8-20 years)

Blanc, French for white

Blanc de Blancs, suffix, indicates that a wine made from only white grapes

Blanc de Noirs, suffix, indicates that a white wine made from only black grapes

Blanquette de Limoux, AC, Languedoc: SW p103

Blanquette Méthode Ancestrale, AC, Languedoc: SW p103

Blayais, see Blaye

Blaye, AC, Bordeaux (Right Bank): W p16 and R p19 (3-7 years)

Bonnes Mares, AC and Grand Cru, Burgundy (Côte de Nuits): R p37 (12-25 years)

Bonnezeaux, AC, Loire: W p57 (8-20 years)

Bordeaux, AC: W p16, R p18 (1-5 years) and P p21

Bordeaux Clairet, AC: P p21

Bordeaux-Côtes-de-Francs, AC, Bordeaux (Right Bank): W p16 (5-10 years) and R p18 (5-10 years)

Bordeaux-Côtes-de-Francs Liquoreux, AC, Bordeaux (Right Bank): W p17 (5-15 years)

Bordeaux Haut-Benauge, AC, Bordeaux (Entre-Deux-Mers): W p16

Bordeaux Rosé, see P Bordeaux

Bordeaux Sec, see W Bordeaux

Bordeaux Supérieur, AC: W p16, R p18 (2-6 years) and P p21

Bordeaux Supérieur Clairet, see Bordeaux Clairet

Bordeaux-Supérieur-Côtes-de-Francs, see Bordeaux-Côtes-de-Francs

Bordeaux Supérieur Rosé, see Bordeaux Supérieur

Bourboulenc, white grape, p46 p49 p96

Bourg, AC, Bordeaux (Right Bank): W p16 and R p19 (3-10 years)

Bourgeais, see Bourg

Bourgogne, AC, Burgundy: W p34 (1-4 years), R p39 (2-5 years) and P p40 (1-4 years)

Bourgogne Aligoté, AC, Burgundy: W p34 (Bouzeron 2-6 years)

Bourgogne Aligoté Bouzeron, see Bourgogne Aligoté

Bourgogne Blanc, see W Bourgogne

Bourgogne Clairet, see P Bourgogne

Bourgogne Clairet Hautes-Côtes de Beaune, see P Bourgogne Hautes-Côtes de Beaune

Bourgogne Clairet Hautes-Côtes de Nuits, see P Bourgogne Hautes-Côtes de Nuits

Bourgogne Grand-Ordinaire, AC, Burgundy: W p34 (1-4 years), R p39 (2-6 years) and P p40

Bourgogne Hautes-Côtes de Beaune, AC, Burgundy (Côte de Beaune): W p32 (1-4 years), R p38 (4-10 years) and P p40

Bourgogne Hautes-Côtes de Nuits, AC, Burgundy (Côte de Nuits): W p32 (1-4 years), R p36 (4-10 years) and P p40

Bourgogne Mousseux, AC, Burgundy: SR p41

Bourgogne Passe-Tout-Grains, AC, Burgundy: R p39 (2-6 years) and P p40

Bourgogne Rosé, see P Bourgogne

Bourgogne Rosé Hautes-Côtes de Beaune, see P Bourgogne Hautes-Côtes de Beaune

Bourgogne Rosé Hautes-Côtes de Nuits, see P Bourgogne Hautes-Côtes de Nuits

Bourgogne Rouge, see R Bourgogne

Bourgueil, AC, Loire: R p60 (6-10 years) and P p63

Bouzeron, sub-appellation of Bourgogne Aligoté

Bouzy, sub-appellation of Coteaux Champenois

Braquet, black grape, p105 p106

Brézème-Côtes-du-Rhône, AC, Southern Rhône: R p48

Brouilly, AC, Beaujolais: R p35 (2-7 years)

Brut, suffix, indicates that a wine is bone dry, usually for sparkling only

Bugey, VDQS, Savoie: W p83, R p85 and P p86

Bugey Cerdon Pétillant, VDQS, Savoie: SP p87

Bugey Mousseux, AC, Savoie: SW p87

Bugey Pétillant, see Bugey Mousseux

Burgundy, English name for Bourgogne

Buzet, AC, Bordeaux satellites: W p16, R p20 (3-10 years) and P p21 (1-4 years)

C

Cabardès, AC, Languedoc: R p98 (3-8 years) and P p100

Cabernet d'Anjou, AC, Loire: P p63

Cabernet Franc, black grape, p18 p19 p20 p21 p60 p63 p67 p89 p92

Cabernet de Saumur, AC, Loire: P p63

Cabernet Sauvignon, black grape, p18 p19 p20 p21 p22 p62 p65 p89 p92

Cadillac, AC, Bordeaux (Entre-Deux-Mers): W p17 (3-8 years)

Cahors, AC, Bordeaux satellites: R p20 (3-12 years)

Canon-Fronsac, AC, Bordeaux (Right Bank): R p18 (7-20 years)

Carignan, black grape, p49 p98-101 p105 p106

Cassis, AC, Provence: W p107, R p105 and P p106

Cerdon, sub-appellation for SP Bugey

Cérons, AC, Bordeaux (Left Bank): W p17 (6-15 years)

Chablis, AC, Burgundy: W p32 (2-6 years)

Chablis Grand Cru, AC, Burgundy: W p32 (6-20 years)

Chablis Premier Cru, AC, Burgundy: W p32 (4-15 years)

Chambertin, AC and Grand Cru, Burgundy (Côte de Nuits): R p36 (12-30 years)

Chambertin-Clos de Bèze, AC and Grand Cru, Burgundy (Côte de Nuits): R p36 (12-30 years)

Chambolle-Musigny, AC, Burgundy (Côte de Nuits): R p36 (8-20 years)

Champagne, AC: SW p79 (prestige cuvées or vintage Champagne can 6-25 years, or 50 years with Blanc de Blancs) and SP p79 (prestige cuvées or vintage 6-25 years)

Chapelle-Chambertin, AC and Grand Cru, Burgundy (Côte de Nuits): R p36 (8-20 years)

Chardonnay, white grape, p32-33 p34 p41 p47 p59 p73 p75 p78-79 p83 p87 p97 p103

Charmes-Chambertin, AC and Grand Cru, Burgundy (Côte de Nuits): R p37 (10-20 years)

Chassagne-Montrachet, AC, Burgundy (Côte de Beaune): W p32 (5-15 years) and R p38 (10-25 years)

Chasselas, white grape, p58 p73 p83

Château, French for castle, most commonly used in Bordeaux to mean estate

Château-Chalon, AC, Jura: W p82

Château Grillet, AC, Northern Rhône: W p47 (3-7 years)

Châteaumeillant, VDQS, Loire: R p61 and P p64

Châteauneuf-du-Pape, AC, Southern Rhône: W p46 and R p49 (6-25 years)

Châtillon-en-Diois, AC, Northern Rhône: W p47, R p50 and P p50

Chénas, AC, Beaujolais: R p35 (3-8 years)

Chenin Blanc, white grape, p56-57 p66 p91 p97

Chevalier-Montrachet, AC and Grand Cru, Burgundy (Côte de Beaune): W p32 (10-20 years)

Cheverny, AC, Loire: W p57, R p61 and P p64

Chignin-Bergeron, sub-appellation of Vin de Savoie, W varietal Roussanne

Chinon, AC, Loire: W p56, R p60 and P p63

Chiroubles, AC, Beaujolais: R p35 (1-8 years)

Chorey-Lès-Beaune, AC, Burgundy (Côte de Beaune): W p32 (3-8 years) and R p38 (7-15 years)

Cinsault, black grape, p49 p50 p98-101 p105 p106

Clairet, suffix, indicates that the wine is a dark pink – this style of wine used to be very common in Bordeaux and resulted in the British word claret to describe red wines from Bordeaux

Clairette, white grape, p46 p52 p96 p97 p107

Clairette de Bellegarde, AC, Languedoc: W p97

Clairette de Die Méthode Dioise Ancestrale, AC, Northern Rhône: SW p52

Clairette du Languedoc, AC: W p97 (8-20 years for rancio)

La Clape, sub-appellation of Coteaux du Languedoc, W based on Bourboulenc

Climat, a named vineyard in Burgundy

Clos du Lambrays, AC and Grand Cru, Burgundy (Côte de Nuits): R p36 (10-20 years)

Clos de la Roche, AC and Grand Cru, Burgundy (Côte de Nuits): R p36 (10-20 years)

Clos St.-Denis, AC and Grand Cru, Burgundy (Côte de Nuits): R p36 (10-25 years)

Clos de Tart, AC and Grand Cru, Burgundy (Côte de Nuits): R p36 (15-30 years)

Clos Vougeot, AC and Grand Cru, Burgundy (Côte de Nuits): R p36 (10-25 years)

Collioure, AC, Roussillon: R p99 (3-15 years) and P p101

Condrieu, AC, Northern Rhône: W p47 (4-8 years)

Corbières, AC, Languedoc: W p96, R p99 (2-5 years) and P p101

Cornas, AC, Northern Rhône: R p48 (7-20 years)

Corse, AC, Corsica: W p109, R p109 and P p109

Corton, AC and Grand Cru, Burgundy (Côte de Beaune): W p33 (10-25 years) and R p38 (12-30 years)

Corton-Charlemagne, AC and Grand Cru, Burgundy (Côte de Beaune): W p33 (5-25 years)

Costières de Nîmes, AC, Languedoc: W p96, R p98 (2-3 years) and P p100

Côt or Cot, see Malbec

Coteaux d'Aix-en-Provence, AC: W p107, R p105 (3-12 years) and P p106

Coteaux d'Ancenis, VDQS, Loire: W p56-58, R p60-62 and P p63-65

Coteaux de l'Aubance, AC, Loire: W p57 (5-10 years)

Coteaux Champenois, AC, Champagne: W p78, R p78 and P p78

Coteaux de Die, AC, Northern Rhône: W p46

Coteaux du Giennois, AC, Loire: W p57, R p61 and P p64

Coteaux du Languedoc, AC: W p96, R p98 (1-4 years) and P p100

Coteaux du Layon, AC, Loire: W p57 (5-15 years)

Coteaux de Loir, AC, Loire: W p56, R p62 and P p65

Coteaux du Lyonnais, AC, Beaujolais: W p34 and R p35 (2-5 years)

Coteaux de Pierrevert, AC, Southern Rhône periphery: W p46, R p49 (2-5 years) and P p50

Coteaux de Quercy, VDQS, Bordeaux satellites: R p20 (2-4 years) and P p21

Coteaux de Saumur, AC, Loire: W p57 (5-10 years)

Coteaux du Tricastin, AC, Southern Rhône periphery: W p46, R p49 (2-7 years) and P p50

Coteaux Varios, AC, Provence: W p107, R p105 and P p106

Coteaux du Vendômois, VDQS, Loire: W p56, R p62 and P p65

Côtes d'Auvergne, VDQS, Loire: W p59, R p61 and P p64

Côte de Beaune, AC, Burgundy: W p32 (3-8 years) and R p38 (10-20 years)

Côte de Beaune Villages, AC, Burgundy: R p38 (7-15 years)

Côtes de Bergerac, AC, Bordeaux satellites: R p20 (3-10 years)

Côtes de Blaye, see Blaye

Côtes de Bordeaux-St.-Macaire, AC, Bordeaux (Entre-Deux-Mers): W p17

Côtes de Bourg, see Bourg

Côtes de Brouilly, AC, Beaujolais: R p35 (3-8 years)

Côtes du Brulhois, VDQS, Bordeaux satellites: R p20 (2-4 years) and P p21

Côtes du Cabardès et de l'Orbiel, see Cabardès

Côtes-Canon-Fronsac, see Canon-Fronsac

Côtes-de-Castillon, AC, Bordeaux (Right Bank): R p18 (5-15 years)

Côte Chalonnaise, district of Burgundy

Côtes de Duras, AC, Bordeaux satellites: W p16, R p20 and P p21

Côtes de Duras Moelleux, see semi-sweet W Côtes de Duras

Côtes du Forez, AC, Loire: R p61 and P p64

Côtes du Frontonnais, AC, SW France: R p89 (2-8 years) and P p92

Côtes du Jura, AC: W p82-83 (vin de paille 10-50 years, vin jeune 10-100 years), R p84-85 (2-8 years, except Trousseau 3-12 years) and P p86

Côtes du Jura Mousseux, see Crémant du Jura

Côtes du Lubéron, AC, Southern Rhône periphery: W p46, R p49 (3-7 years) and P p50

Côtes de la Malapère, VDQS, Languedoc: R p98 (3-7 years) and P p100

Côtes du Marmandais, AC, Bordeaux satellites: W p16, R p20 (2-5 years) and P p21

Côtes de Millau, VDQS, SW France: W p91, R p89 and P p92

Côtes de Montravel, AC, Bordeaux satellites: W p17 (3-8 years)

Côte de Nuits, district of Burgundy in Côte d'Or

Côte de Nuits Villages, AC, Burgundy: W p32 (1-4 years) and R p36 (6-10 years)

Côte d'Or, district of Burgundy

Côtes de Provence, AC: W p107, R p105 (3-10 years) and P p106

Côtes-du-Rhône, AC: W p46, R p49 (2-8 years) and P p50

Côtes-du-Rhône-Villages, AC, Southern Rhône: W p46, R p49 (3-10 years) and P p50

Côtes Roannaises, AC, Loire: R p61 (1-5 years) and P p64

Côte Rôtie, AC, Northern Rhône: R p48 (10-25 years)

Côtes du Roussillon, AC: W p97, R p99 (3-8 years) and P p101

Côtes du Roussillon Villages, AC: R p99 (3-15 years)

Côtes du St.-Mont, VDQS, SW France: W p90, R p89 (2-5 years) and P p92

Côtes de Toul, AC, Lorraine: W p70-72, R p74 and P p74

Côtes du Ventoux, AC, Southern Rhône periphery: W p46, R p49 (2-5 years) and P p50

Côtes du Vivarais, AC, Southern Rhône periphery: W p46, R p48 and P p50

Counoise, black grape, p49 p51

Courbu, white grape, p90

Cour-Cheverny, AC, Loire: W p59

Crémant d'Alsace, AC: SW p75 (5-8 years) and SP p75 (3-5 years)

Crémant de Bordeaux, AC: SW p22 and SP p22

Crémant de Bourgogne, AC, Burgundy: SW p41 (3-7 years) and SP p41 (2-5 years)

Crémant de Die, AC, Northern Rhône: SW p52

Crémant du Jura, AC: SW p87

Crémant de Limoux, AC, Languedoc: SW p103

Crémant de Loire, AC: SW p66 and SP p67

Crépy, AC, Savoie: W p83

Criots-Bâtard-Montrachet, AC and Grand Cru, Burgundy (Côte de Beaune): W p33 (8-20 years)

Crozes-Hermitage, AC, Northern Rhône: W p47 and R p48 (6-20 years)

Cru Bourgeois, a classification system for the châteaux of Médoc which were not included in the original 1865 cru classé list

Cru Classé, indicates that the château was included in the original 1865 classification for red wines of Médoc and Graves (p. 32-33), or sweet W wines of Sauternes and Barsac (p. 25)

D

Demi-Sec, suffix, French for semi-dry, although actually indicates that a wine is off-dry to medium

Domaine, French for estate, equivalent of château most commonly used in Burgundy

Doux, suffix, indicates that a wine is sweet
Duras, black grape, p93

E

Échezeaux, AC and Grand Cru, Burgundy (Côte de Nuits): R p37 (10-20 years)
Edelzwicker, AC, Alsace: W p72
Entre-Deux-Mers, AC, Bordeaux: W p16
Entre-Deux-Mers-Haut-Benauge, see Entre-Deux-Mers
L'Étoile, AC, Jura: W p82-83 (vin de paille 10-50 years, vin jeune 10-100 years)
L'Étoile Mousseux, AC, Jura: SW p87

F

Faugères, AC, Languedoc: R p98 (3-10 years) and P p100
Fer, black grape, p20 p89 p92
Fiefs Vendéens, VDQS, Loire: W p56, R p62 and P p65
Fitou, AC, Roussillon: R p99 (3-6 years)
Fixin, AC, Burgundy (Côte de Nuits): W p32 (3-8 years) and R p36 (6-20 years)
Fleurie, AC, Beaujolais: R p35 (2-8 years)
Floc de Gascognes, AC, an apéritif made from unfermented grape juice and Armagnac brandy, serve very cold
Folle Blanche, white grape, p59
Fronsac, AC, Bordeaux (Right Bank): R p18 (6-15 years)
Frontignan, see Muscat de Frontignan
Fuella, black grape, p105 p106

G

Gaillac, AC, SW France: W p91 (doux 5-15 years), R p89 and P p92

Gaillac Doux, see sweet W Gaillac
Gaillac Mousseux Méthode Deuxième Fermentation, AC, SW France: SW p93 and SP p93
Gaillac Mousseux Méthode Gaillaçoise, AC, SW France: SW p93 and SP p93
Gaillac Mousseux Méthode Gaillaçoise Doux, see sweet Gaillac Mousseux Méthode Gaillaçoise
Gaillac Premier Côtes, AC, SW France: W p91 (2-5 years)
Gamay, black grape, p35 p39 p40 p41 p49 p50 p51 p61 p62 p64 p65 p74 p86 p84 p85 p89 p92
Gevrey-Chambertin, AC, Burgundy (Côte de Nuits): R p37 (7-20 years)
Gewürztraminer, white grape, p70 p72
Gigondas, AC, Southern Rhône: R p48 (7-20 years) and P p50 (2-5 years)
Givry, AC, Burgundy: W p32 (3-8 years) and R p39 (5-12 years)
Grand Cru, French for great growth, the highest designation of climat in Burgundy and Champagne, used more loosely elsewhere
Grand Cru Classé, indicates an officially classified château in St-Émilion
Grand Echézeaux, AC and Grand Cru, Burgundy (Côte de Nuits): R p37 (10-20 years)
Grand Marque, French for great brand, and until recently a select group of top Champagne houses
La Grand Rue, AC and Grand Cru, Burgundy (Côte de Nuits): R p37 (7-15 years)
Grand Vin, suffix used in Bordeaux, French for great wine, although actually only indicates that this is the top wine from this particular château

Graves, AC, Bordeaux (Left Bank): W p16 and R p19 (2-15 years)

Graves Supérieur, AC, Bordeaux (Left Bank): W p17 (6-15 years)

Graves de Vayres, AC, Bordeaux (Entre-Deux-Mers): W p16 and R p18 (4-10 years)

Grenache (Noir), black grape, p48 p49 p50 p98-101 p102 p105 p106

Grenache Blanc, white grape, p46 p51 p96

Grenache Gris, pink grape, p51

Griottes-Chambertin, AC and Grand Cru, Burgundy (Côte de Nuits): R p36 (10-20 years)

Grolleau, black grape, p65

Gros Manseng, white grape, p90

Gros Plant, VDQS, Loire: W p59

H

Haut-Médoc, AC, Bordeaux (Left Bank): R p19 (5-8 years, rising to 6-15 years for Cru Classé except Château La Lagune 10-30 years)

Haut-Montravel, see Côtes de Montravel

Haut-Poitou, VDQS, Loire: W p57-59, R p60-62 and P p63-65

Hermitage, AC, Northern Rhône: W p47 (6-12 years, except vin de paille 10-30 years) and R p48 (12-30 years)

Hermitage Vin de Paille, see Hermitage

I

Irancy, AC, Burgundy: R p39 (2-5 years)

Irouléguy, AC, SW France: W p90, R p89 (4-10 years) and P p92

J

Jacquère, white grape, p84

Jasnières, AC, Loire: W p57

Juliénas, AC, Beaujolais: R p35 (3-8 years)

Jurançon, AC, SW France: W p90 (sec 2-5 years, sweet 5-20 years)

Jurançon Noir, black grape, p20

Jurançon Sec, see dry W Jurançon

K

Klevener de Heiligenstein, AC, Alsace: W p73

L

Ladoix, AC, Burgundy (Côte de Beaune): W p32 (4-8 years) and R p38 (7-20 years)

Lalande-de-Pomerol, AC, Bordeaux (Right Bank): R p18 (7-20 years)

Latricères-Chambertin, AC and Grand Cru, Burgundy (Côte de Nuits): R p36 (10-20 years)

Len de l'El, white grape, p91 p93

Libournais, district of Bordeaux which includes St.-Émilion and Pomerol

Limoux, AC, Languedoc: W p97

Liquoreux, suffix, indicates a wine so sweet as to be liqueur-like

Lirac, AC, Southern Rhône: W p46, R p49 (4-10 years) and P p50

Listrac, AC, Bordeaux (Left Bank): R p19 (5-10 years)

Listrac-Médoc, see Listrac

Lladoner Pelut, black grape, p98-100

Loupiac, AC, Bordeaux (Entre-Deux-Mers): W p17 (5-15 years)

Lussac-St.-Émilion, AC, Bordeaux (Right Bank): R p18 (5-12 years)

M

Macabéo, white grape, p96 p97 p99 p101

Mâcon, AC, Burgundy: W p32 (1-4 years), R p35 (2-6 years) and P p40

Mâcon Supérieur, AC, Burgundy: W p33 (1-4 years), R p35 (3-8 years) and P p40

Mâcon Villages, AC, Burgundy: W p33 (1-4 years)

Mâconnais, district of Burgundy south of Côte d'Or

Macvin, AC, an aperitif made from unfermented grape juice and marc, which is a spirit like Italian grappa that is made from grape skins

Madiran, AC, SW France: R p89 (5-15 years)

Malbec, black grape, p18 p19 p20 p21 p62 p98

Maranges, AC, Burgundy (Côte de Beaune): W p32 (4-8 years) and R p38 (2-7 years)

Marcillac, AC, SW France: R p89 (3-6 years) and P p92

Margaux, AC, Bordeaux (Left Bank): R p19 (5-10 years, rising to 5-20 years for cru classé except premier and deuxième cru classé 10-25 years)

Marignan, sub-appellation of Vin de Savoie, W varietal Chasselas

Marsannay, AC, Burgundy (Côte de Nuits): W p32 (3-8 years), R p37 (4-10 years) and P p40

Marsannay La Côte, see Marsannay

Marsanne, white grape, p46 p47 p49 p51 p53

Maury, AC, Roussillon: F p102 (10-30 years)

Mauzac, white grape, p46 p49 p51 p91 p97 p103

Mazis-Chambertin, AC and Grand Cru, Burgundy (Côte de Nuits): R p37 (10-20 years)

Mazoyères-Chambertin, see Charmes-Chambertin

Mazy-Chambertin, see Mazis-Chambertin

Médoc, AC, Bordeaux (Left Bank): R p19 (4-8 years)

Melon (de Bourgogne), white grape, p58

Menetou-Salon, AC, Loire: W p57, R p61 (2-5 years) and P p64

Mercurey, AC, Burgundy: W p33 (3-8 years, 5-15 years for premiers crus) and R p39 (5-12 years)

Merlot, black grape, p18 p19 p20 p21 p22 p62 p89 p92 p98

Meursault, AC, Burgundy (Côte de Beaune): W p32 (5-15 years) and R p38 (8-20 years)

Meursault-Blagny, see W Meursault

Minervois, AC, Languedoc: W p96, R p98 (1-5 years) and P p100

Moelleux, suffix, French for soft, although actually indicates that a wine is medium-sweet

Molette, white grape, p84

Monbazillac, AC, Bordeaux satellites: W p17 (7-20 years)

Mondeuse, black grape, p86 p84 p85

Mondeuse Blanche, white grape, p84

Montagne-St.-Émilion, AC, Bordeaux (Right Bank): R p18 (5-15 years)

Montagny, AC, Burgundy: W p33 (3-10 years, 4-12 years for premiers crus)

Monthélie, AC, Burgundy (Côte de Beaune): W p33 (4-8 years) and R p38 (7-20 years)

Montlouis-sur-Loire, AC, Loire: W p57 (2-10 years)

Montlouis-sur-Loire Mousseux, AC, Loire: SW p66

Montlouis-sur-Loire Pétillant, AC, Loire: SW p66

Montrachet, AC and Grand Cru, Burgundy (Côte de Beaune): W p33 (10-30 years)

Montravel, AC, Bordeaux satellites: W p16

Morey-St.-Denis, AC, Burgundy (Côte de Nuits): W p32 (3-8 years) and R p36 (8-20 years)

Morgon, AC, Beaujolais: R p35 (4-9 years)
Moselle, VDQS, Lorraine: W p70-73 and R p74
Moulin-à-Vent, AC, Beaujolais: R p35 (4-9 years)
Moulis, AC, Bordeaux (Left Bank): R p19 (5-12 years)
Moulis-en-Médoc, see Moulis
Mourvèdre, black grape, p49 p50 p98-101 p105 p106
Mousseux, suffix, French for sparkling and indicates that a wine is fully sparkling
Mousseux de Savoie, AC: SW p87
Müller-Thurgau, white grape, p73
Muscadelle, white grape, p16 p17 p22 p91
Muscadet, AC, Loire: W p58
Muscadet Côtes de Grandlieu, AC, Loire: W p58
Muscadet Coteaux de la Loire, AC: W p58
Muscadet de Sèvre-et-Maine, AC, Loire: W p58
Muscat, white grape, p51 p52 p71 p72 p102 p109
Muscat de Beaumes-de-Venise, AC, Southern Rhône: F p51
Muscat du Cap Corse, AC, Corsica: F p109
Muscat de Frontignan, AC, Languedoc: F p102
Muscat de Lunel, AC, Languedoc: F p102
Muscat de Mireval, AC, Languedoc: F p102
Muscat de Rivesaltes, AC, Roussillon: F p102
Muscat de St.-Jean-de-Minervois, AC, Languedoc: F p102
Musigny, AC and Grand Cru, Burgundy (Côte de Nuits): W p32 (8-20 years) and R p37 (10-30 years)

N
Négrette, white grape, p89 p92
Nielluccio, black grape, also known as Sangiovese in Italy, p109
Nouveau, suffix synonymous with Primeur, indicating any new wine – not just Beaujolais Nouveau – that may be sold from the third Thursday of November, to be drunk young
Nuits, see Nuits-St.-Georges
Nuits-St.-Georges, AC, Burgundy (Côte de Nuits): W p32 (5-10 years) and R p37 (7-20 years)

O
Ondenc, white grape, p91
Orléans-Cléry, VDQS, Loire: R p60

P
Pacherenc du Vic-Bilh, AC, SW France: W p90 (3-7 years)
Pacherenc du Vic-Bilh Doux, see sweet W Pacherenc du Vic-Bilh
Pacherenc du Vic-Bilh Moelleux, see semi-sweet W Pacherenc du Vic-Bilh
Pacherenc du Vic-Bilh Sec, see dry W Pacherenc du Vic-Bilh
Palette, AC, Provence: W p107, R p105 (7-20 years) and P p106
Patrimonio, AC, Corsica: W p109, R p109 and P p109
Pauillac, AC, Bordeaux (Left Bank): R p19 (5-12 years, rising to 10-25 years for cru classé except premier and deuxième cru classé 10-30 years)
Pécharmant, AC, Bordeaux satellites: R p20 (4-12 years)
Pernand-Vergelesses, AC, Burgundy (Côte de Beaune): W p33 (4-8 years) and R p38 (7-20 years)

Pessac-Léognan, AC, Bordeaux (Left Bank): W p16 (3-8 years, rising to 5-20 years for cru classé) and R p19 (6-20 years)

Pétillant, suffix, indicates that a wine is lightly sparkling, less than mousseux

Petit Verdot, black grape, p19

Pétillant de Savoie, see Mousseux de Savoie

Petit Chablis, AC, Burgundy: W p32

Petit Manseng, white grape, p90

Picpoul, white grape, p46 p51 p96

Picpoul-de-Pinet, sub-appellation of Coteaux du Languedoc

Pic-St-Loup, sub-appellation of Coteaux du Languedoc

Pineau d'Aunis, black grape, p62 p65

Pineau des Charentes, AC, an apéritif made from unfermented grape juice and Cognac, serve very cold

Pinot Blanc, white grape, p34 p41 p46 p49 p51 p58 p72 p73

Pinot Gris, pink grape, p58 p65 p71

Pinot Meunier, black grape, p62 p74 p78-79

Pinot Noir, black grape, p36-39 p40 p41 p61 p62 p64 p65 p74 p75 p78-79 p86 p84 p85

Pomerol, AC, Bordeaux (Right Bank): R p18 (5-10 years, rising to 10-30 years for top châteaux)

Pommard, AC, Burgundy (Côte de Beaune): R p38 (8-20 years)

Pouilly-Fuissé, AC, Burgundy: W p33 (3-8 years)

Pouilly-Fumé, AC, Loire: W p57 (2-5 years)

Pouilly-Loché, AC, Burgundy: W p33 (1-4 years)

Pouilly-sur-Loire, AC: W p58

Pouilly-Vinzelles, AC, Burgundy: W p33 (1-4 years)

Poulsard, black grape, p86 p84 p87

Premier Cru, French for first growth, the second highest designation of climat in Burgundy and Champagne, used more loosely elsewhere

Premier Cru Classé, the highest classification of cru classé

Premières Côtes de Blaye, AC, Bordeaux (Right Bank): W p16 and R p19 (4-10 years)

Premières Côtes de Bordeaux, AC, Bordeaux (Entre-Deux-Mers): W p17 (3-7 years) and R p18 (4-8 years)

Primeur, suffix synonymous with Nouveau, indicating any new wine that may be sold from the third Thursday of November and to be drunk young

Puisseguin-St.-Émilion, AC, Bordeaux (Right Bank): R p18 (5-10 years)

Puligny-Montrachet, AC, Burgundy (Côte de Beaune): W p32 (5-15 years) and R p38 (10-20 years)

Q

Quarts-de-Chaume, AC, Loire: W p57 (5-15 years)

Quincy, AC, Loire: W p57

R

Rancio, suffix, wines that have been exposed in their barrels to heat and air, which gives them a distinctive nutty/melted butter smell

Rasteau, AC, Southern Rhône: F p51 (1-5 years)

Régnié, AC, Beaujolais: R p35 (2-7 years)

Reuilly, AC, Loire: W p57, R p61 (2-5 years) and P p65 (2-5 years)

Richebourg, AC and Grand Cru, Burgundy (Côte de Nuits): R p37 (12-30 years)
Riesling, white grape, p70 p72
Ripaille, sub appellation of Vin de Savoie, W varietal Chasselas
Rivesaltes, AC, Roussillon: F p102 (10-20 years)
La Romanée, AC and Grand Cru, Burgundy (Côte de Nuits): R p37 (12-30 years)
Romanée-Conti, AC and Grand Cru, Burgundy (Côte de Nuits): R p37 (15-35 years)
Romanée-St.-Vivant, AC and Grand Cru, Burgundy (Côte de Nuits): R p37 (10-25 years)
Romorantin, white grape, p59
Rosé, suffix, French for pink
Rosé d'Anjou, AC, Loire: P p65
Rosé d'Anjou Pétillant, see P Anjou Pétillant
Rosé des Riceys, AC, Champagne: P p78
Rosé de Loire, AC: P p63
Rosette, AC, Bordeaux satellites: W p17 (4-8 years)
Rouge, suffix, French for red
Roussette du Bugey, VDQS, Savoie: W p83
Roussanne, white grape, p46 p47 p49 p51 p53 p83
Roussette du Bugey, AC: W p83
Roussette de Savoie, AC: W p83
Ruchottes-Chambertin, AC and Grand Cru, Burgundy (Côte de Nuits): R p36 (8-20 years)
Rully, AC, Burgundy: W p33 (3-8 years, 5-12 years for premiers crus) and R p39 (5-12 years)

S

Sacy, white grape, p59
St.-Amour, AC, Beaujolais: R p35 (2-8 years)

St.-Aubin, AC, Burgundy (Côte de Beaune): W p33 (3-10 years) and R p38 (4-15 years)
St.-Bris, AC, Burgundy: W p34 (2-5 years)
St.-Chinian, AC, Languedoc: R p98 (2-6 years) and R p100
St.-Croix-du-Mont, AC, Bordeaux (Entre-Deux-Mers): W p17 (5-15 years)
St.-Émilion, AC, Bordeaux (Right Bank): R p18 (5-15 years, rising to 10-20 years for premier grand cru classé B and 12-35 years for premier grand cru classé A)
St.-Émilion Grand Cru, see St.-Émilion
St.-Estèphe, AC, Bordeaux (Left Bank): R p19 (5-12 years, rising to 10-25 years for cru classé)
Ste.-Foy-Bordeaux, AC, Bordeaux (Entre-Deux-Mers): W p16 (3-7 years) and R p18 (3-7 years)
St.-Georges-St.-Émilion, AC, Bordeaux (Right Bank): R p18 (5-15 years)
St.-Joseph, AC, Northern Rhône: W p47 and R p48 (3-8 years)
St.-Julien, AC, Bordeaux (Left Bank): R p19 (5-12 years, rising to 6-20 years for cru classé except deuxième cru classé 10-25 years)
St.-Nicolas-de-Bourgueil, AC, Loire: R p60 (5-10 years) and P p65
St.-Péray, AC, Northern Rhône: W p47
St.-Péray Mousseux, AC, Northern Rhône: SW p53
St.-Pourçain, VDQS, Loire: W p59, R p62 and P p65
St.-Romain, AC, Burgundy (Côte de Beaune): W p33 (3-7 years) and R p38 (4-8 years)
St.-Véran, AC, Burgundy: W p33 (1-4 years)

Sancerre, AC, Loire: W p57 (2-5 years), R p61 and P p64

Santenay, AC, Burgundy (Côte de Beaune): W p33 (4-10 years) and R p38 (7-15 years)

Saumur, AC, Loire: W p56 and R p60 (1-10 years)

Saumur-Champigny, AC, Loire: R p60 (5-10 years)

Saumur Mousseux, AC, Loire: SW p66 (3-5 years) and SP p67

Saumur Pétillant, AC, Loire: SW p66

Saussignac, AC, Bordeaux satellites: W p17 (5-15 years)

Sauternes, AC, Bordeaux (Left Bank): W p17 (6-30 years, rising to 20-60 years for Château d'Yquem)

Sauvignon Blanc, white grape, p16 p17 p22 p34 p57 p90 p91 p93

Savagnin, white grape, p82 p87

Savagnin Rosé, pink grape, p73

Savennières, AC, Loire: W p56 (5-8 years)

Savigny, see Savigny-Lès-Beaune

Savigny-Lès-Beaune, AC, Burgundy (Côte de Beaune): W p33 (4-15 years) and R p38 (7-20 years)

Sciacarello, black grape, p109

Sec, suffix, indicates that a wine is dry

Sélection de Grains Nobles, suffix used in Alsace, indicates a sweet wine from grapes affected by noble rot

Sémillon, white grape, p16 p17 p22 p91

Seyssel, AC, Savoie: W p83

Seyssel Mousseux, AC, Savoie: SW p87

Supérieur, suffix, used in Bordeaux and Burgundy to indicate a higher level of alcohol

Sur Lie, suffix particularly used for Muscadet, indicates that the wine has spent a winter on its yeast sediment, which adds further depth of flavour

Sylvaner, white grape, p72 p73

Syrah, black grape, p48 p49 p50 p89 p92 p98-100

T

La Tâche, AC and Grand Cru, Burgundy (Côte de Nuits): R p37 (12-30 years)

Tannat, black grape, p20 p89 p92

Tavel, AC, Southern Rhône: P p50

Terroir, French for soil, although it is taken to mean the combination of soil, micro-climate and appropriately matched grape varieties

Touraine, AC, Loire: W p56-57, R p60-62 and P p63-65

Touraine-Amboise, AC, Loire: W p56, R p60 and P p63

Touraine Azay-le-Rideau, AC, Loire: W p57 and P p64

Touraine-Mesland, AC, Loire: W p56, R p60 and P p63

Touraine Mousseux, AC, Loire: SW p66, SR p67 and SP p67

Touraine Pétillant, AC, Loire: SW p66, SR p67 and SP p67

Tourbat, white grape, p97

Trousseau, black grape, p86 p84

Tursan, VDQS, SW France: W p90 (2-5 years), R p89 (2-5 years) and P p92

U

Ugni Blanc, white grape, p46 p49 p51 p96 p107 p109

V

Vacqueyras, AC, Southern Rhône: W p46, R p49 (4-12 years) and P p50

Valençay, VDQS, Loire: W p59, R p60 and P p63

VDP, see Vin de Pays

VDQS, see Vin Délimité de Qualité Supérieure

Vendange, French for harvest

Vendange Tardive, suffix used in Alsace, French for late harvest, indicates a sweet wine made from fully ripe grapes that were picked later

Vermentino, white grape, p46 p109

Vielles Vignes, French for old vines, no consistent definition

Vin, French for wine

Vin d'Alsace , see Alsace

Vin d'Alsace Edelzwicker, see Edelzwicker

Vin de Bandol, see Bandol

Vin de Bellet, see Bellet

Vin de Corse, see Corse

Vin Délimité de Qualité Supérieure, or VDQS, the second highest level in the French wine classification system, below Appellation d'Origine Controlée and above Vin de Pays

Vin Doux Naturel, French for naturally sweet wine, where brandy is added before all sugar is turned to alcohol

Vin de Frontignan, see Muscat de Frontignan

Vins d'Entraygues et du Fel, VDQS, SW France: W p91, R p89 and P p92

Vins d'Estaing, VDQS, SW France: W p91, R p89 and P p92

Vin Gris, suffix, French for grey wine, indicates that the wine is a very light pink

Vin Jaune, suffix, French for yellow wine, where wine has been left to oxidise in cask, which turns it yellow-gold and gives it a distinctive sherry-like character

Vin Jeune d'Arbois, see Arbois

Vin Jeune de l'Étoile, see l'Étoile

Vins de Lavilledieu, VDQS, SW France: W p91 and R p89 (3-6 years)

Vins de l'Orléanais, VDQS, Loire: W p58-59, R p60 and P p63

Vin de Paille, suffix, French for straw wine, where grapes have been dried on straw mats and make a very sweet complex wine

Vin de Paille d'Arbois, see Arbois

Vin de Paille de l'Étoile, see L'Étoile

Vin de Pays, the third highest level in the French wine classification system, below VDQS and above Vin de Pays

Vin de Savoie, AC: W p83, R p84-85 (2-8 years) and P p86

Vin de Savoie d'Ayze Mousseux, AC: SW p87

Vin de Savoie d'Ayze Pétillant, see Vin de Savoie d'Ayze Mousseux

Vin de Savoie Mousseux, see Mousseux de Savoie

Vin de Savoie Pétillant, see Mousseux de Savoie

Vin de Table, the lowest level in the French wine classification system, below Vin de Pays

Vins du Thouarsis, VDQS, Loire: W p56, R p60 and P p63

Viognier, white grape, p46 p47 p49

Viré-Clessé, AC, Burgundy: W p33 (1-4 years)

Volnay, AC, Burgundy (Côte de Beaune): R p38 (6-20 years)

Vosne-Romanée, AC and Grand Cru, Burgundy (Côte de Nuits): R p37 (10-20 years)

Vougeot, AC, Burgundy (Côte de Nuits): W p32 (4-10 years) and R p37 (8-20 years)

Vouvray, AC, Loire: W p56 (doux 5-50 years)

Vouvray Mousseux, AC, Loire: SW p66

Vouvray Pétillant, AC, Loire: SW p66

ABOUT US

Hugh Baker

Without wine, Hugh would never have met his wife Penny. It is a long story, but suffice to say he owes a lot to this drink. Exploring the infinite variety of wine started with wine tastings at Cambridge University, and developed into a voracious hobby and an enduring passion.

Hugh is a consultant with Booz Allen Hamilton. Having spent much of his adult life stretching his mind around the operational problems facing some of the world's largest companies, he is now using his strangely analytical brain to untangle the world of wine. His day job has taken him to all corners of the globe and has given him the opportunity to taste a wide variety of wines.

Hugh lives and works in London.

cracking.it

cracking.it is a publishing company. We believe that many of life's pleasures can be improved upon with a bit of knowledge. However, many of these pleasures have been around long enough to evolve into something really complicated.

We also believe that understanding the system behind the pleasure helps you to remember what you like, and gives you the confidence to explore further and enjoy more.

cracking.it is dedicated to explaining the systems behind pleasures, so they may be enjoyed more. If you would like to be kept informed of our future developments, please:

Visit us online at: www.cracking.it

E-mail us at: info@cracking.it

Write to us at: cracking.it
                         74 Wycliffe Road
                         London SW11 5QR
                         United Kingdom

ACKNOWLEDGEMENTS

This book has taken four years to bring into being, and would not have grown from its original incarnation as a kitchen poster without the encouragement and cajoling of many people.

Special thanks for this go to my beloved wife Penny, Caz Hildebrand, Dalia Balz, Fabri Kramer, Joe Dolce, Mark Paton, Patrick Walsh, Jake Pearce and Bex Ganz, Paul Kitcatt, Charlie and Sandra Towers-Clark, Richard Stark, Julian Copeman, James Cowling, Nick Allen and Huw Williams. And thank you too for reading this book.

The contents of this book are the tip of an iceberg of information about French wines. I am particularly grateful to L'Institut National des Appellations d'Origine, and the authors of the following books:

- **The Sotheby's Wine Encyclopedia**, by Tom Stevenson
- **The New France**, by Andrew Jefford
- **Wines of Bordeaux**, by David Peppercorn
- **Bordeaux, the Comprehensive Guide**, by Robert Parker
- **Wines of Burgundy,** by Serena Sutcliffe
- **The Great Domaines of Burgundy**, by Remington Norman
- **Drink!**, by Susy Atkins and Dave Broom
- **Vines**, Grapes & Wines, by Jancis Robinson
- **Hugh Johnson's Pocket Wine Book**
- **The World Atlas of Wine**, by Hugh Johnson & Jancis Robinson
- **Hachette Wine Guide**
- **The Oxford Companion to Wine**, by Jancis Robinson
- **The Wine Book**, by Matthew Jukes